THE CHANGING F

Ann Spokes Symonds

Robert Boyd
PUBLICATIONS

CW00688709

Published by
Robert Boyd Publications
260 Colwell Drive
Witney, Oxfordshire OX8 7LW

First published 1999

Copyright © Ann Spokes Symonds and
Robert Boyd Publications

ISBN: 1 899536 41 8

All rights reserved. No part of this book may be produced, stored in a retrieval system, or transmitted, in any form or by any means, electronic, mechanical, photocopying, recording or otherwise, without the prior approval of the publisher.

TITLES IN THE *CHANGING FACES* SERIES

Banbury: Book One
The Bartons
Bicester: Book One *and* Book Two
Bladon with Church Hanborough and
    Long Hanborough
Botley and North Hinksey: Book One
    and Book Two
Chipping Norton: Book One
St Clements and East Oxford:
    Book One *and* Book Two
Cowley: Book One, Book Two *and*
    Book Three
Cowley Works: Book One
Cumnor and Farmoor with Appleton
    and Eaton
St Ebbes and St Thomas: Book One
    and Book Two
Eynsham: Book One *and* Book Two
Faringdon and District
Grimsbury
Headington: Book One *and* Book Two
Iffley
Jericho: Book One *and* Book Two
Kennington
Littlemore and Sandford

Marston: Book One *and* Book Two
North Oxford: Book One *and* Book Two
Oxford City Centre: Book One
South Oxford: Book One *and* Book Two
Summertown and Cutteslowe
West Oxford
Witney: Book One
Wolvercote with Wytham and Godstow
Woodstock: Book One *and* Book Two
Yarnton with Cassington and Begbroke

FORTHCOMING
Abingdon
Banbury: Book Two
Blackbird Leys
Charlbury
Cowley Works: Book Two
Easington
Florence Park
Grimsbury: Book Two
Littlemore and Sandford: Book Two
Oxford City Centre: Book Two
Rose Hill
Thame
Witney: Book Two

Printed and bound in Great Britain at The Alden Press, Oxford

Contents

Front cover picture

May Day in Iffley in about 1900, courtesy of Iffley Women's Institute.

Back cover picture

Iffley Church

Acknowledgements

I should like to thank all those who gave me such a friendly welcome while I was working on this book and for their willingness to provide me with information and photographs and to answer my queries. I have acknowledged any photographs used. However, there are others who kindly gave me help and advice, including:

Mrs Verena Allen, Mr Jonathan Allen, Mr John Ashdown, Miss Charlotte Banks, Mrs Lena Barrett, Mr Andrew Benfield, Mrs Mary Bennett, Mrs Thelma Bennett, Mr and Mrs Ron Bromley, Mr Tom Collis, Mrs I Crisp, Mrs Joan Critchley, the late Mr John Critchley, Mr Jeremy Daniel, Mr Carol Davis, Professor Peter Dickson, Miss Sheila Fairfield, Mrs Kay Firman, Mrs Gelder, Mr Bill Gibbs, Mrs E Gilpin, Miss Edith Gollnast, Dr Malcolm Graham, Mrs Graham Greene, Mrs Freda Hoare, the late Mrs Bronwen Huntley, Mrs Noony Knowles, Mr John Knox, Mrs Angie Langridge, *Oxford Mail and Times* Library, the Reverend Richard Lea, the late Mrs G Low, Mrs Joyce Marchant, Miss Betty Mayall, Professor and Mrs D Nineham, Miss Celia Palmer, the late Mr Gerald Palmer, Mrs Pam Parker, Mr David Penwarden, Mr John Perrott, Mr John Phipps, Mr Keith Price, Picture Editor, *Oxford Mail and Times,* Mr and Mrs Patrick Reynolds, Mr Tom Rose, Mrs Jean Russell, Mr and Mrs Edwin Townsend-Coles, Dame Joan Varley, Mr Geoff Wakeham, Mrs D Ward, the late Dr Kathleen Warin, Mr Ralph Wyatt, Lady Yardley.

My grateful thanks also go to my husband Richard Symonds for helping me with my research, for reading proofs and also for all his encouragement. I could not have managed without the computer skills of Dr Desmond Walshaw and the invaluable advice and help in connection with my own photographs given to me by Dr Milo Shott. Thanks also go to the staff of 'Mail Boxes Etc' in Summertown for their laser-printing skills, also Geoff Parkinson for his efficient sub-editing.

Every effort has been made to trace all the copyright holders but I was unsuccessful in the case of one photograph and hope that anyone claiming copyright will please get in touch with me.

Ann Spokes Symonds

NOTE ON THE PHOTOGRAPHS

Some of the original photographs were faded or unsharp and did not reproduce well but I have included some of these for historical reasons or to illustrate a point. I hope that readers will therefore forgive the quality in order that they can at least gain some impression and be able to appreciate the atmosphere of the place, group or event.

Introduction

The name Iffley has been spelled more than 84 different ways since the earliest written evidence of Gifetelea in 941. This proves that the roots of Iffley go down deep. There is certainly evidence of Bronze Age occupation, an urn having been found on the river bed. Implements made by pre-historic man have also been found there.

The origin of the name is uncertain but suggestions include 'field of gifts' or 'plovers' clearing'. A Dr Guest is quoted in Edward Marshall's *Account of the Township of Iffley,* written in 1870, 'In a case of so much difficulty [over the name] it is more prudent, as it is certainly the more honest course, to confess one's ignorance.'

In the Domesday Book (1086) the village was called 'Givetelei' and other variants have been Yiftele (1201), Zesterley (1234) and Yetley (1517). Leonard Hutten, a Canon of Christ Church, writing in the 17th century asks the reader : 'on leaving Hinksey on the left hand, [to] cast your eye downeward over the Water, and you shall see a Towne, called Ifley, knowne especially by that title, that the Parsonage thereof is the peculiar corps of the Archdeaconry of Oxford.' By the 18th century the name was spelled as it is today.

A verse of 1793, possibly written by John Skinner of Trinity College, includes:

'At Folly Bridge we hoist the sail
And briskly scud before the gale
To Iffley — where our course awhile
Detain — its locks and Saxon pile
Affording pause.'

The original parish was larger than the present one and included not only Iffley township (sometimes called Church Iffley) but part of Littlemore (also called little Iffley) and Hockmore Street (otherwise known as Middle Cowley).

At the time of Edward the Confessor Iffley was held by Azor, a Saxon chief. Then it became the property of Earl Albric of Aubrey until about the time of Domesday. In 1393 Sir Edward Abberbury, some-time guardian to Richard III, near to death, wished to fund a 'hospital' for poor men at his manor of Donnington in Berkshire. He was licensed to set this up and endow it with the Manor of Iffley. From then onwards Iffley belonged to the Trustees of the hospital.

The Oxford to London Road via Iffley was turnpiked in 1736. From the 16th to the 19th century most of the inhabitants were occupied in farming, although there were also many well-to-do families who had pursuits and interests in Oxford as well. By 1852 four farmers, a sheep dealer, a corn dealer and a miller were recorded (in Gardener's *Directory*) but 75 years later there was only one farm and a single market garden which had any commercial interest in the land.

The fields were enclosed in 1830. By 1841 the population was 764 and the residential character of the village had become established. In Gardener's 1852 *Directory* the village was described as 'romantically situated on the banks of the Isis 2 miles SE by S of Oxford.' By the Extension Act of 1928 part of the parish was included in the City of Oxford and the remainder added to Littlemore. Up to 1912 horse buses ran to Iffley Town. Main drainage was completed and gas installed in 1906, electricity in 1925 and the first telephone in 1912. Street lighting did not come until 1920 and even by 1930 was somewhat sparse.

In 1925 an American, by the name of Robert R. Tristram Coffin, wrote a book about Iffley and in a chapter called 'Iffley the Unspoiled' wrote: 'somehow unconsciously people there seemed to have learned the art of living. Tending their roses, living just as they please behind their high garden walls, leaving their hearts open to their open fires, getting the singing of their tea-kettles into their souls . . .'

By 1949, Reginald Turner wrote: 'Iffley at least has some honourable identity. It is off the main road, there is an island on the Isis and the Norman Church is a masterpeice'. However, he concluded that on the edge of the village 'suburbia sprawls indecently.' In 1948, at the time when Thomas Sharp wrote *Oxford Replanned,* it was intended to construct a by-pass cutting off the old village of Iffley from the rest of the City. 'Certainly,' wrote Sharp, 'this road passing so close to Iffley will not in any way improve it. But it will save it from extinction'. And because no new building would have been allowed south or west of the road it would 'act as a barrier, as a breakwater which will keep back suburban floods that even now are about to overtake the old village.' The idea was that Iffley would be isolated from suburbia. In the event, the plans were changed even before Sharp's book went to press because of the need to build more houses in the Rose Hill area.

In the late 1960s there were yet more plans to put roads through Iffley which meant that residents feared that it would cease to be a cul de sac and thus spoil its character as a village. Eventually the City Council erected posts in order to prevent motor traffic travelling between the two communities of Iffley and Rose Hill.

In an article in the *The Oxford Times* on 1st July, 1966, it was stated that the reason the Donnington Trust was selling the building land it owned in Iffley was because of 'continual objections to its development plans.' The Trust's surveyor and agent, Mr Martin French, was quoted as saying; 'We had hoped to develop Iffley as a very high-class village but the opposition makes this impossible.'

By the time the *Encyclopedia of Oxford* was published in 1988 Iffley was described as 'a small village within the City beleaguered by suburbia' and mention was made of the pace of suburbanisation quickening dramatically since 1971. Helen Turner, later to become Secretary of the Oxford Preservation Trust, said that Iffley was 'fighting a rearguard action for its very existence.' It has been a Conservation Area since 1969 (extended in 1985) but it was also described (in 1977) as the hardest hit of all Oxford's Conservation Areas.

Nevertheless, the village of Iffley, which in 1999 had an electorate of nearly 800, has retained its separateness and rural charm and one can at least say that much of the infilling could have been worse. It is also a comparatively peaceful village with no through traffic as there was in times gone by.

The prize-winning Iffley Scrap Book compiled, in the 1950s, by members of the Iffley Women's Institute (see Section 10) described Iffley as 'a friendly village where newcomers are soon made at home, children and adults greet each other, little groups, not only of housewives, gossip in the street, dogs are friendly, pleasant chat beguiles the waiting customers of all three shops . . . Most of us would not change our home to any other place.'

Today it is still a friendly, welcoming place and those who live here are happy with their choice.

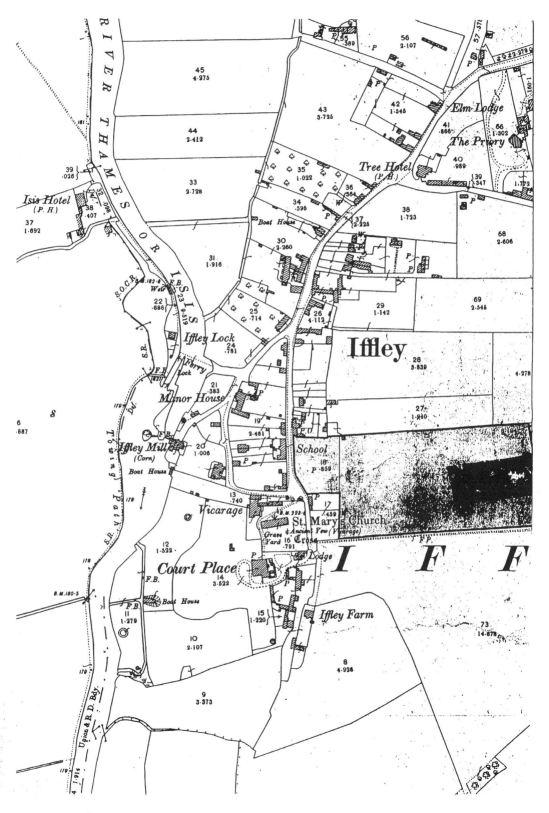

The Centre of Iffley. Reproduced with permission from the 1899 Ordnance Survey Map.

A view of Iffley village taken in 1955. Copyright Areofilms and published with their permission.

Architectural Heritage

Iffley has a wealth of houses of merit, some of which were standing four centuries ago. At least 17 houses are listed as being of architectural or historical interest and most of these are illustrated in this book.

Tudor Cottage (No. 56 Church Way). Once known as Donnington Cottage, it was built in the 16th/17th century. At one time it was a restaurant. Tudor Close has been built in the grounds.

The interior of Tudor Cottage when it was a tea room (courtesy of Dr Kathleen Warin). It is now a private house.

The interior of Tudor Cottage. The parlour showing the ancient bread oven (courtesy of Dr Kathleen Warin).

Furry inhabitants of the oven.

The Thatched Cottage is probably early 17th century although the casement windows are modern and there were major alterations in 1965. Situated on the corner of Mill Lane and Church Way, it was originally three cottages of slightly different dates.

Alice Smith, the benefactress, who in her will of 1678 bequeathed land to the poor of Iffley, lived here. In the early days some of the money was used for apprenticing poor children.

Dame Joan Varley, whose mother, Mrs Fleetwood Varley, lived here for about 20 years, tells me that the cottage was reputed to be haunted. Few villagers would go in after dark and the Varleys could never get anyone to help at dinner parties. Certainly there were ghosts about in the village. The Women's Institute Scrap Book of 1955 records that no one dared to walk along the lane between the churchyards for fear of encountering the Nun or the Headless Knight said to haunt the area. A peg-legged phantom was encountered up to at least 1947 although he was usually heard — with the traditional clanking of chains — rather than seen.

The Thatched Cottage can be seen on the right in this photograph taken in about 1906. (Copyright Jeremy's, Oxford Stamp Centre).

The Manor House and Rosedale in Mill Lane.The top photograph shows them before alterations in 1919 and the lower one in 1921 afterwards.

The Manor House, once Lincoln Farmhouse, substantially 17th century in origin but with a mordernised exterior, was once the home of the Nowells (see Section 5). Boswell wrote about a visit: *'Dr Johnson and I went in Dr Adams' coach to dine with Dr*

Nowell, Principal of St Mary Hall, at his beautiful villa at Iffley on the banks of the Isis. We were well entertained and very happy . . . where was a very agreeable company: We drank 'Church and King' after dinner with true Tory cordiality,'.

Unfortunately, the whole of the south wing was burnt down in October, 1810 when Captain (later Vice-Admiral) Nowell was living there. It was thought to be the work of arsonists.

Rosedale, the house on the right, was built by the Donnington Trust on the site of the burnt-out wing and they are two separate buildings. (Photographs by courtesy of Mrs. Joyce Marchant.)

Rosedale has a most attractive garden as can be seen in these photographs taken in 1930 (see Section 10) (courtesy of Mrs Joyce Marchant) and in 1999.

Builders at work on a new house in front of the Manor House and Rosedale. (Courtesy of *Oxford Mail and Times*).

Beechwood (listed Grade II) is late 18th century and has its own drive leading from Iffley Turn. The house now belongs to All Souls College who have built flats in the grounds. Dr John Sparrow, the Warden of All Souls from 1952 to 1977, who was a great Oxford character, went to live here in retirement.

The actress Rosina Filippi (Mrs Henry Martin Dowson) (1866–1930) lived here from at least 1900. On the bank at the rear of the house she produced plays (usually Shakespeare) in which the local children acted. Another family, the William Fosters, who lived there from the First World War until the 1920s, staged musicals on the same bank. Mrs Violet Webb, who would have been seven years old in 1913, tells me that Mrs Foster always insisted that she curtsy to her. The owner in the 1930s was Major General Christopher Reginald Buckle, CB, CMG, DSO.

Mr and Mrs Kenneth Knowles lived there for 12 years from 1954. Mrs Noony Knowles was founder and a Chairman of the Friends of Iffley. She remembers that soon after they first moved in, an elderly Colonel called regularly at the house to see how it was getting on because he had once lived there. Noony kept reminding him that he had left his hat on a peg in the house and it was waiting for him to collect it. However, he always declined to take the hat, perhaps wishing that something of himself should remain for ever at Beechwood.

Grove House, Iffley Turn, is early 19th century, rendered and painted, with a cast-iron verandah and a trellis canopy. It is listed Grade II. In the 1830s, it was known as Sadler's House after a farmer who lived there. It also has a coach house, where horses were once stabled, but the stalls now house coal, kindling and logs. Mrs Jemima Newman, mother of Cardinal John Newman (1801–1890) lived here when he was Vicar of St Mary the Virgin, Oxford. She came to this house in 1830 and died there in 1836. There is a plaque giving this information which can be seen in the photograph (taken in April, 1999) beside the left-hand ground-floor window. Mrs Newman's two daughters lived with her and one wrote to her brother, John Henry, about the house: 'I could never wish for anything nicer or prettier'.

The house was at one time called Rose Bank and when the curate of St Giles, James Rumsey, lived there he was visited by the Reverend Charles Dodgson, (Lewis Carroll) (1832–1898). Carroll's brother, the Reverend E H Dodgson, was curate of Iffley in 1904/5. By 1900 the house was owned by Henry Carter (see Section 10).

Another owner of Iffley Turn House (as it was then called) was Sir George William Forrest (1845–1926) who was a local benefactor. It was he who gave the first building which housed the Memorial Institute to the village in 1918 (see Section 7). Once a week Sir George and Lady Forrest would roll up the red carpet in their drawing-room so that the youth of the village could have dancing lessons. Afterwards, Lady Forrest (who continued to live at the house after the death of her husband) would provide cakes and coffee. Sir George had been born in India, worked for the Indian Government, and was a distinguished writer of India's history, including the well-known *The History of the Indian Mutiny.* He was knighted in 1913 for services to India.

During the Second World War the writer Shi I. Hsuing (born 1902) was living at the house. In 1935 he wrote the popular play *Lady Precious Stream.* The house by then belonged to Colonel Wilfred House, Fellow of the Queen's College, who later became Headmaster of Wellington School. It was from him that Mrs Graham Greene (wife of the writer) (see Section 10) bought the house and grounds in 1947 for £10,000. Both house and garden had been much neglected and she had to replace floors, ceilings and fireplaces. There was not even a telephone. The garden was completely wild, with hares in the long grass, and one of Mrs Greene's cats brought in a baby hare as a gift offering. Fortunately, she was able to take the hare back where it came from. Mrs Greene (Vivien) renamed the place Grove House.

In 1962 Mrs Graham Greene built a rotunda in the garden of Grove House in which to keep and display some 50 dolls' houses which she had started to collect in 1944. The collection was on weekly display until it was sold in 1998.

Wood House.

All that remains of this 19th century house, which was demolished after a fire in 1964, is the name of the road (now spelled as one word) which links Iffley Turn and Tree Lane and was built in 1987/98. It was once the home of Charles Mostyn Owen (1819–1894), Chief Constable of Oxfordshire, after his retirement.

In this photograph of Wood House can be seen the mounting block used by Edward VII when Prince of Wales. He lodged his staff and stabled his horses here when he was an undergraduate at Oxford. The Prince often attended services at Iffley Church where, according to Henry Taunt, the photographer, there was no ceremony or fuss. He was usually accompanied by

either Major Teesdale or Canon Duckworth. He did not stay for the sermon, pleading that if he remained he would be late for the service at the Cathedral. Bay Tree Court was built on the site of the house and Aubrey Court on its paddock.

Legend has it that under this stone pine tree at Wood House Sir John Stainer (1840–1901), Professor of Music at Oxford University, composed the oratorio *The Crucifixion.* His son Charles lived at Wood House between 1918 and 1930. Before that it was the home of the well-known Oxford surgeon, E A Bevers, MRCS, JP.

A cartoon of Sir John Stainer by 'Spy'
in *Vanity Fair.*

Field House, No. 113 Church Way. There is a plaque on the house with the date 1741. At
one stage it was a tavern and old bottles have been dug up from time to time in the
garden. It was once a post office kept by the Misses Blay and for a period, until the mid-
1960s, it bore the name 'Sunnyside'.

The Priory, off the east side of Church Way is listed Grade II. It was probably built about 1840–50 with later additions and has a stucco front and gothic traceried windows. This photograph was taken in the 1990s and is reproduced by courtesy of Mrs Maria Hardman.

IFFLEY APRIL 26 1908   [A S]

Iffley, Oxford

Two views of Church Way looking south. The snow fell on an unseasonable 26th April in 1908. The other picture was taken about the same year. Rivermead, probably of 17th century origin, is on the right with the gabled porch. It has a 19th century addition, 18th century sash and casement windows and is listed Grade II. The house was bought by the Reverend Joseph F Phelps in 1914 and the Misses Phelps lived there well into the 1940s (see Section 9). Violet Webb (née Polley), born in 1906, who lived at Nowell House further down the road, remembers the two Phelps sisters as 'very Victorian ladies.' Francis Phelps, son of Joseph, was Archbishop of Cape Town in the 1930s.

Iffley is so blessed with old houses that it is not possible to include pictures of them all. Both Nowell House and Court House can be seen in Section 5. The attractive pink Townsend House (called Elm Lodge in 1875 and the Lodge in 1895) gives striking interest to the corner of Church Way and Meadow Lane. Malthouse Cottages and Malthouse have merit and the name reminds one of the trade of maltster carried on in earlier times. The latter was at one time called Isis Bank. It was once the home of Mr John Millington Sing who became Warden of St Edward's School, Oxford.

Other houses of interest include Denton House, once a preparatory school for boys and where Charles Reade, the novelist, went as a pupil. Wootten was the home of Montague Wootten, the banker and then of Mr John Allen before he moved to the Elms.

The Elms (see Section 8) was at one time occupied by Mr J Bickerton, Town Clerk of Oxford, and his family. Lucia House was once the home of Miss Jane Lenthall, a very good friend of the village children, but who also embarked on so many lawsuits against her neighbours that she died penniless. It was later occupied by Miss Grayson.

There has been much infilling and new development over the last 25 years, some of which have been built on the gardens or fields of larger houses. One of the more extensive developments is Aubrey Court, three blocks of 18 flats by the architects Gray and Baynes for Cherwell Housing Trust, which was built in 1981. The Domesday Book records that from 1066 onwards Lord Aubrey held Iffley from the King. It was so named by Oxford City Council in April, 1979. Bay Tree Close consists of 14 houses by P Reynolds and Partners, built by J Rendell in 1981. Azor's Court is made up of 17 single-storey units for elderly people, called after the Saxon Lord of Iffley, and designed by D Kelvey for Oxford City Council in 1981.

In Stone Quarry Lane, 13 houses, designed by the Peter and Diane Bozeat Partnership for Iffley Self-Build Housing Association, were erected in 1980–81. Sheepway Court, (1981) consisting of 19 dwellings, designed by P Reynolds and Partners for J Rendell, is named after sheepway furlong, situated at the south of Tree Lane, and also commemorates the medieval sheepway on the line of the present Tree Lane which is said to have continued as far as Shotover. In Bear's Hedge, situated off Tree Lane, Oxford City Council built 19 houses designed by M Gregory. It is named after a travelling and performing bear. He and his minder often rested in a hedge in the vicinity of this development.

Lucas Place and Remy Place were built in six blocks of flats for elderly people and designed by Peter del Nevo for Oxford Citizens' Housing Association and Alice Smith Charities. They were built in 1975. Fitzherbert Close is a development of 10 houses designed by Oxford Architects Partnership for Norman Collisson (Contractors Ltd.) in about 1971. Four houses were added later. The Chairman of the Donnington Trustees at the time the Close was built is connected to the Fitzherbert family.

Hartley Russell Close consists of four flats for elderly people, built by J Carter Jonas for the Donnington Hospital Trust in 1951. It was named after one of the Trust's Patrons. Grove Court in Church Way was designed by Oxford Architects Partnership. The information about these new developments was kindly given by Mr John Ashdown, Conservation Officer, Oxford City Council.

Cordrey Green. The photograph shows part of it, taken in April, 1999. It consists of 14 houses by I R Brooks and Company, built for Crown House Properties (Oxford) Ltd. in 1980. It is named after Edward Cordrey (1884–1972), the Iffley historian

and benefactor, who grew up in the village. (See Section 10.)

Above: Iffley House (taken in 1990), built in the grounds of Denton House, was designed by the City Architect of the time (1963), Douglas Murray, to accommodate 60 elderly people. It was described by Pevsner as 'an impressive design'. In 1974 it came under the control of Oxfordshire County Council. Anne Grennwood Close, the name given to the Close behind Denton House, was named after a voluntary nurse at Iffley House.

A modern addition to the street scene erected by British Telecom and being made use of not only by a member of the public but by a feline resident. It is in Church Way and was taken in 1999.

The Church

'At Iffley, one of the most exquisite Norman Churches in England stands in a hush by the river'.

Jan Morris   *'Oxford'*

The Church of St Mary the Virgin in 1765 from the north-east. It was probably built about 1172–82 by the Norman Lord of the Manor, Robert de St Remy, in the reign of Henry II (1154–1189). It is a characteristic late Norman Romanesque parish church and most of the original building survives to this day. A yew tree, reputed to be 1500 years old, still stands in the churchyard. The print is courtesy of the Vicar of Iffley. The three fine doorways (north, west and south) are all original Norman.

The first clergyman is recorded in about 1170. From 1208 until 1225 Kenilworth Priory held the living but from that date the Archdeacons of Oxford, and now Christ Church, have held the patronage. At one time the Vicar was known as the 'Perpetual Curate' because it was the Archdeacon who had the sole right in and control of the benefice. This title is not used today.

Annora de Braose, the Anchorite, inhabited a walled-up cell attached to the Church from 1232. Hugh Mortimer, her husband, had died in 1227 and there were no children. Henry III sent her firewood and a cloak to keep her warm.

The Church in 1834 showing the west doorway. All writers about it are effusive about its looks. Edward Marshall wrote in 1870 that every book on English architecture of that time made some mention of Iffley Church. Jennifer Sherwood, writing in *A Guide to the Churches of Oxfordshire,* describes it as 'small but gorgeously decorated. The ornament is magnificent.' Pevsner and Sherwood chose Iffley Church to adorn the cover of their *Guide to Oxfordshire* and called it 'one of the most complete village churches.' The magnificent chestnut tree which stands by the gate of the churchyard was planted by the Reverend Edward Marshall (Vicar) in the 1820s.

The fenced-off west door as it was in 1808.

The west door today with its elaborate carving. The circular rose window had already replaced the three-paned window, shown in the 1834 print, in about 1857.

Iffley Church today showing both west and south doors. The south doorway has even more elaborate carving than the west.

Two of the gargoyles which are the work of the sculptor Michael Groser. They were carved at the time the tower was restored in 1975.

If there had been an invasion of England by the Germans in the Second World War the bells of all the churches were to ring out to give the alarm. On one occasion the Iffley bells were rung by mistake and there was panic in the village. The Air Raid wardens went round knocking up all the men asking them to come out.

Right: The interior of the church in a print of 1834. By the mid-13th century the chancel had been extended. In 1738 a singers' gallery was built at the west end. Alterations were made to the church in 1844 and throughout the 19th century from time to time. The position of the pulpit was changed and in 1995 it was removed altogether. Preachers now use a portable lectern from which they can see the whole congregation.

Left: The interior in 1999 taken from approximately the same position as in the print above. Note the thinner pillars made of black marble from Tournai in Belgium, the same material from which the font was made.

Right: The black marble font dates from when the church was built except for one of the supporting pillars which is 13th century, It has a round hollow deep enough for total immersion. (Courtesy Miss Betty Mayall)

The second font, which is medieval and listed Grade II, can be seen in this photograph taken at a baptism in the 1970s, outside the west doorway. There is a legend that a farmer once 'borrowed' this font, after it had been dug up in the churchyard, to use as a drinking trough for his cows. When they would have nothing to do with it he returned it. It has been in its present position since 1962. The church was being restored when the Vicar, the Reverend Jonathan Hills, baptised the granddaughter of Mrs Lena Barrettt, a long-time resident of the village. The girl, at the age of 10, decided it was about time she was baptised. (Courtesy Mrs Lena Barrett).

This south-west window was designed by John Piper and made by David Wasley. It had remained in Piper's studio until his death in 1992 and was given in his memory by his widow Myfanwy. It was dedicated on 23rd June, 1996.

Because the original design was smaller than the Iffley window, Wasley added the bottom panel with the agreement of the Piper family. The quotation *'Let man and beast appear before Him and magnify His name together...'* is from *'Rejoice in the Lamb'* by Christopher Smart (1772–1771). The background is a brilliant dark blue, characteristic of many Piper windows. The golden cockerel sings *'Christ is born'* and the leaves of the tree which supports the birds are in bright reds, greens and yellows. The drawing is by Mrs G Low and is reproduced with her kind permission.

Iffley Rectory from the top of the Church tower in 1970 before the passages and porch shown in the foreground were removed by the Landmark Trust. Listed Grade II★, the south range of the main north-south block is probably 13th century with the north range added in the 16th century and the east wing in the 17th century. It has some fine 17th century panelling inside. That part of the Rectory which stands directly on Mill Lane is now known as the Parsonage and is let out by the Landmark Trust. (Photograph courtesy of Iffley Church.)

Iffley Church and the Rectory taken in 1999. The Church is a lively place today, filled with a large congregation of all ages at the regular Sunday services.

Court Place

'It was hardly an exaggeration when a man of taste and discernment recently said that ours was the finest house in Oxford . . . for my part I want this to be my last earthly home.'

Sir Alan Gardiner who lived at Court Place 1947–1963.

One only has to look at the Ordnance Survey map of 1899, reproduced on page 7, to realise what importance was attached to Court Place, indicating that it was the largest estate under the manor. It originally had 11 acres of land and there was a small area of farmland there which was attached until 1955.

Two views of Court Place as it was in 1999, the exterior of which has changed little in the last 200 years. Although there is a gabled wing on the south-east which appears to be 17th century, most of the house was built in the late 18th century. A re-set stone on the north side gives '1580 I L' for John Lewys, which indicates a possible earlier building.

Although Court Place is atttractive enough, it is its position high up on the banks of the River Thames, known here as the Isis, which is its main advantage. The house is of course listed of special architectural and historical interest, Grade II. It is believed that the old manor courts were held here.

There have been many distinguished inhabitants of Court Place since Vice-Admiral William Nowell moved there in 1810 after the Manor House in which he had lived was set on fire. William was the nephew of Sarah and Thomas Nowell (see Section 5). Nowell had joined the Navy at 14 and once quelled a mutiny by running below decks, grabbing the ringleader and knocking him out. He married Rosamina Brett and they had five children, three of whom were born in Iffley. He died in 1828 and on the death of his widow in 1841 the family left the village.

Henry Walsh, solicitor, was tenant from 1841 until his death in 1869 and James Richard Mallam had it from 1869. Records between 1869 and 1889 are patchy but in about 1889, until his death in 1906, Major Frederick Nash Ind lived there. In that same year the American evangelist Hannah Whitall Smith, (Mrs Pearsall Smith) and her son Logan came to live at Court Place.

Hannah Pearsall Smith (1832–1911), seen here with her two daughters, Mary and Alys, in 1898. Her parents, the Whitall Smiths, were Philadelphia Quakers and her father a wealthy glass manufacturer. Hannah was a remarkable woman and we are fortunate to be able to get a flavour of her character from her published letters and some biographical sketches by her granddaughter. Writing under the pen name 'H.W.S.', one of Hannah's books *The Christian's Secret of a Happy Life,* brought her world fame, not only with a wide circulation in the United States of America and Britain but it was translated into both European and Oriental languages. At the age of 19 Hannah had married Robert Pearsall Smith. In 1873 he left the USA for England where he became a well-known preacher. She and her three children joined him the following year. They were Mary (born 1864), Logan and Alys (born 1867). Hannah's success as a preacher was said to have been equal to her husband's. In fact she was adored everywhere she went and because of her beauty was known as 'the angel of the churches'. She later took up Temperance work, being against both alcohol and tobacco. Her husband died in 1898 and in 1906, at the age of 73, she and her son Logan leased Court Place.

Hannah, who by this time was confined to what she called 'a wheeled chair' obviously found the house and grounds to her liking. There were then about eight acres, with some splendid trees, including a Cedar of Lebanon, and fine views of the river (nowadays obscured by trees and scrub). She said that she often had the feeling of living in a novel. When she received callers in the drawing room with its many large windows she said that she felt like a 'fasting man in a glass case on show.' When one of her daughters accused her mother of being 'County' she replied that 'County never called Iffley gentry.' In any case she was indifferent to class.

Hannah thought that visiting was a waste of time. Soon after her arrival she wrote: 'Another caller! Here [compared with London] it is all surface talk which I hate'. Six months later she complained: 'Again callers have hindered my writing. I believe Iffley people spend their lives paying calls.' On one occasion, though, she was pleased to have 'nearly converted a visitor to Women's Suffrage'. A consolation was that because of her physical condition she was not expected to return calls. One day a lady came to call and was so overcome to find that it was *the* Mrs Whitall Smith that she fell down on her knees, kissed her hand and wept. Hannah wrote to her daughter Mary: 'I really began to feel some sympathy with God with the worship he has to put up with so often.'

By October, 1906 Hannah already suffered from the cold and wore three vests. By winter she had added more vests, a corset, a corset cover and a velveteen bolero jacket, making eight coverings in all. By then 'she felt like an animated cushion as if pins might be stuck in me.'

One day she had a lesson in not knowing what is good for us. The Donnington Trustees had sold some trees to a lumber merchant including two which bordered her view of the river and a little white bridge. It was across this bridge which her daughter Alys, who was married to Bertrand Russell, bicycled every day from Bagley Wood to Court Place to see her mother. Hannah 'moved Heaven and Earth' to prevent the trees being pulled down and was forced to give up in despair, feeling like a martyr. 'But lo and behold' she admitted that she found she had an even more lovely view of the river 'and would not have had them put back for anything.'

Left: Alys, Hannah's younger daughter, with her husband Bertrand Russell, taken in 1907.

Although not an Anglican, Hannah seems to have been friends with the Vicar next door at the Rectory. On one occasion when he was away she looked after his canary and hid his silver under her son Logan's bed. Mary, Hannah's oldest child, had left her husband Francis Costelloe, a barrister, in 1891 and had gone off with the art connoisseur, Bernard Berenson. Costelloe made it clear in his will that he wanted the children, who had been baptised Catholics, to keep their religion. Hannah, who, after their father's death, had the girls made wards of court, made sure that they had a Catholic education.

Right: Ray (born 1887) and her younger sister Karin, They became Hannah's reason for living. When they were young she described them as 'little angels of goodness ... who were never naughty unless grown ups made them so.' Later, they were a constant joy to her, spending their holidays from school or college at Court Place. The feeling was obviously mutual. At nine

years old one of them said how much she liked the way her grandmother's mouth was always turned up in a smile.

Ray later graduated from Cambridge and was actively involved in the law-abiding arm of the Suffrage movement. It was said that it was mainly due to her that the movement kept in the public eye despite the more 'flamboyant reputation' of Emmeline Pankhurst. In 1911 Ray married Oliver Strachey, the brother of G. Lytton Strachey. She acted as Secretary to Nancy (Viscountess) Astor and stood for Parliament as an Independent. During the time that the Pearsall Smiths lived in Iffley, they often had visitors of note. One was William James, (the brother of the writer Henry) whose book *Principles of Psychology* was read throughout the world. After that he wrote religious books with equal success and finally turned to philosophy and made Pragmatism famous. The poet and philosopher George Santayana (1863–1952), a pupil of James, also visited Court Place. Part of his 1935 novel *The Last Puritan* is situated in pre-1919 Iffley. Other guests included Virginia Woolf and Lady Otteline Morrell, friends of the Pearsall Smith daughters. Virginia's younger brother, Adrian Stephen, married Karyn Costelloe and Otteline Morrell's daughter married the son of Vinagradoff (see below).

Logan Pearsall Smith (1865–1946), right, taken in 1886 at the age of 21, was equally well known in his own right. Coming from Harvard University to Balliol he was a favourite of Benjamin Jowett who was appreciative of his conversational skills to break the silence on social occasions when groups of shy academics were tongue-tied. With his friend Robert Bridges and others, Logan started the Society for Pure English and several of his books concentrated on the subject of language and its words and idioms. Beatrice Webb described him as a 'refined and good-natured bachelor behind whose smile is a deep melancholy due to a long record of self-conscious failure to become an artist in words.' Barbara Strachey, his great niece, related that 'we made a curious  household. Uncle Logan talks to fill the silences not because he has anything to say. Granny never talks unless she has something to say.' Logan was a lover of Oxford and would often travel there in his launch from Iffley. He remained a bachelor.

After the death of his mother, Logan's sister Alys, by then separated from her husband, Bertrand Russell, came to live at Court Place but it was not long before they moved to London. Alys played an active part in the evolution of Fabianism.

I am indebted to Mrs Barbara Halpern for the photographs of Hannah Pearsall Smith and her children, and also for information from her book *Remarkable Relations*, by Barbara Strachey.

When the Pearsall Smiths left Iffley in 1911 the house was occupied by Sir Paul Vinogradoff (see page 33), who was a legal and constitutional historian. Born in Russia, he had held the chair of history at Moscow University from the age of 16 but resigned when the Government would allow no autonomy and expected professors to report on the political views of their students. He had therefore come to Oxford where in 1903 he became Corpus Professor of Jurisprudence and lived at first in North Oxford.

During the 1914–18 War, he visited Russia to encourage the Government to remain in the War on the Allies' side. He was knighted in 1917 and renounced his Russian

Sir Paul Vinogradoff (1854–1925).

citizenship in 1918. Unfortunately, he lost his money in the Russian Revolution and had to move from Court Place. He had hoped that Russia could have become a constitutional monarchy. His marriage to a Norwegian whose mother was British brought him much happiness. They had a daughter, Helen, who was an opera singer, and a son Igor. On moonlight nights Helen used to sing in the garden of Court Place and her beautiful voice could be heard all over the village

Vinagradoff spoke 12 languages fluently. H A L Fisher, in his memoir of him, said that 'he moved about the world ... with the sense of serene and untroubled composure of a man who finds every country his familiar home' and that 'he stood high with his contemporaries of the civilised world.'

Vinagradoff died in Paris of pneumonia caught at a reception held in his honour. Although his body was buried there his heart came home to rest in Holywell Cemetery where the inscription on his tomb, recognising his appreciation of the welcome he received as a guest of Britain, can be seen today with the words: *HOSPITAE BRITANNIAE GRATUS ADVENA* (A stranger grateful to be a guest of Britain).

Towards the end of the First World War, Court Place became for a time a convalescent home for wounded American officers. Mrs Dulcie Sassoon from London was for a while a sub-tenant.

In about 1919, the Favargers came to Court Place. Henri was an architect and FSA and designed hotels near the Pyramids and at Aswan in Egypt. He died in 1922 at the age of 66 but his widow Anna continued to live at Court Place until about 1937. It is said that she paid for electric lighting in the church in memory of her husband.

John Norman Bryson (1896–1976) owned Court Place from 1939. Born in Belfast, his family were wealthy linen manufacturers. He was a Fellow, Dean and Librarian of Balliol College and tutor in English literature. He was not only a bachelor don of the old school but was an internationally respected connoisseur in the field of music, art and the theatre. His large art collection ranged from Degas to Picasso and he bequeathed his unique collection of Pre-Raphaelite drawings to the Ashmolean Museum.

At Bryson's Memorial Service, Sir John Betjeman, a friend for 50 years, gave the address and described him as a man 'of few words and long friendships'. His circle of friends extended far beyond Oxford University. Betjeman, in a letter, wrote 'With the death of my old friend I feel that the last reader for whom I was writing has disappeared.'

Dr Kenneth Garlick, his former pupil and later Keeper of Western Art at the Ashmolean Museum, wrote that Bryson had 'a wide range of experience of what was going on in the world of music in all the capitals of Europe. Opera was his passion.' He was also a founder of the Playhouse in Oxford.

John Bryson.

After leaving Court Place, he lived at Belsyre Court on the Woodstock Road. (Photograph taken in the 1930s courtesy of Dr K Garlick.)

Left: Richard Addinsell (from Joyce Grenfell's book *Joyce Grenfell Requests the Pleasure*). He was a friend of John Bryson who invited him to stay at Court Place when his London home was bombed in 1940. It was at Court Place that Addinsell composed the theme of *The Warsaw Concerto* for the film *Dangerous Moonlight*. The film and the tune were some of the most popular at that time. Early in 1942 Richard Addinsell was introduced to the actress and singer Joyce Grenfell (1910–1976) on the steps of the National Gallery and soon afterwards they started a long profesional partnership, he composing the music for nearly all her lyrics. As Joyce Grenfell said of *The Warsaw Concerto*: 'It was famous and had been a favourite with the troops and in particular the RAF . . . The theme was played by concert pianists, dance-band pianists and by ear on lamentable canteen uprights the length and breadth of Great Britain and it was continually broadcast.' She said: 'When singing with a pianist of Richard's calibre the intoxication is without measure'. Mrs Madge Webber who, with her husband, kept the village shop (replaced by the Clinic) before managing the Tree Hotel, tells me that Joyce Grenfell and Richard Addinsell would often come in to buy provisions when they were staying in Iffley at weekends.

In 1947 Sir Alan and Lady Gardiner became the new owners of Court Place. After a delay caused by the record heavy snowstorms early that year, they arrived from Hampshire.

Back in 1906 Gardiner had been elected to the Laycock Studentship of Egyptology at Worcester College. He became such an authority on Egypt that he was offered the Professorship of Egyptology at Oxford in 1934. This, however, he refused, suggesting that it should go to a colleague. Gardiner records in his memoirs the day in 1922 when his friend Carnarvon 'telephoned me at Lambourn Road (his home at the time) saying that he had just received a telegram from Carter in Luxor that he had made a wonderful discovery in the Valley, a magnificent tomb with seals intact. Carnarvon asked

Gardiner whether it could by chance be the tomb of Tutankhamun. Some weeks later Gardiner joined Carnarvon and Carter at the tomb where his skill as a decypherer of hieroglyphs was essential to the interpretation of the treasures. Sir Alan was the first, or at least one of the first, to enter the shrine, the Holy of Holies of Tutankhamun. Later he told his head gardener at Court Place, Tom Collis, that he dropped down twenty feet into the tomb but fortunately landed on his feet. He looked around him and everything he saw was gold.

Sir Alan Gardiner (copyright Griffith Institute, Ashmolean Museum).

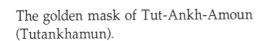

The golden mask of Tut-Ankh-Amoun (Tutankhamun).

When Cecil Mottishaw, Gardiner's butler, who had been with him since 1946, died seven years later, Tom Collis had the task of waking Sir Alan every morning and running his bath. They became friends and once Sir Alan, on the spur of the moment, went to London and came back with a watch as a present for Tom.

The Collis family in front of the old Court Farm cottages which were later demolished by the University. After Sir Alan died in 1963 Tom Collis worked for the University at Court Farm. At the back is Tom Collis. Left to right in front are Charles Collis, Shiela Collis (daughter) and Emily Collis. The family came with Sir Alan to Court Place as he insisted that no one should be without a place to go to when they left Hampshire.

Tom Collis in 1999 outside his home in Azor's Court, Iffley.

Heddie, Lady Gardiner, who was Finnish, was, as Sir Alan recorded 'naturally horrified at the condition of Court Place when she saw it. Permits to reconstruct the back of the house were at first refused but at last the kitchens were made habitable.' Sir Alan would work for long hours in his study and was 'not to be disturbed' whilst Lady Gardiner would take her small dog for walks by the river, proceeding via the toll-gate and paying her penny toll to Bert Cunnington the keeper. The house, in the end, was ideal for Heddie because she suffered a severe stroke in 1955 which deprived her of speech and meant that she became practically bedridden. With a devoted carer in Mrs Henson and night nurses she enjoyed her time in a cheerful bedroom with its own bathroom.

In 1962, the year before his death, Sir Alan felt that Egypt had become 'too much vulgarised' and he had no urge to go back. He thought Abu Simbel could not be saved but felt more valuable antiquities were being neglected. In his will Sir Alan indicated that he would like the University of Oxford to have Court Place.

After Sir Alan's death his executors asked Oxford University whether they would be interested in acquiring Court Place before it was put on the market. The University Estates Committee reported that they thought Court Place would be a suitable purchase with particular reference to a graduate centre. In fact, so enthusiastic were the University that the Curators of the University Chest agreed, in July, 1964, to purchase Court Place for £28,000.

Two graduate colleges for academics who were not attached to other colleges were to be set up and St Cross College and Iffley College were duly established and Fellows appointed. Although the former had by the summer of 1965 both a site and a Principal, there was some delay in finding a Principal of Iffley College. The first person who was asked took nearly six months to consider and then finally turned it down. It was then that the Iffley Fellows expresssed a hope that Sir Isaiah Berlin, Fellow of All Souls and distinguished man of arts and letters, should be offered the Principalship. As he was at the time lecturing at Princeton University, the Vice-Chancellor wrote to him, in November, 1965 and ten days later Berlin cabled to say that he was interested. In the event he took a long time to make up his mind. Many of his friends warned him against accepting, one even suggesting that he would be 'utterly miserable' at Iffley. Berlin also had worries about where the money for the college was to come from.

By December, 1965 the Fellows of Iffley College began to have doubts about the Court Place site and once 'Cherwell', the Haldane's house in North Oxford, became available they suggested that it would be a more suitable place for a graduate college. Court Place was, for instance, twice as far from the Bodleian Library as 'Cherwell'. By July, 1966 the Wolfson Foundation had given the colllege (re-named Wolfson) £1.5 million, the North Oxford site was made available and Berlin had accepted the Presidency.

The University retained Court Place and graduate accommodation, in the form of houses, was built in the grounds. These are now known as Court Place Gardens with access off Rivermead Road, Rose Hill. There is pedestrian access from Iffley village.

(Information from the Oxford University Archives, with their kind permission, and the biography of Sir Isaiah Berlin by Michael Ignatieff (London, 1998).)

The River, Lock and Water Mill

Iffley, an attractive village, is even more enhanced by the river. It stands on a promontory above the Thames, known at this point as the Isis. In earlier days the river was used as much for trade as for leisure as this 19th century print (courtesy of Iffley Church) shows. Even into the early years of the 20th century traffic went by river barges.

The position of the village in relation to the Isis can be seen in this photograph which was probably taken in the 1930s (courtesy of Miss Betty Mayall). The lock and lock-keeper's house can be clearly seen in the foreground.

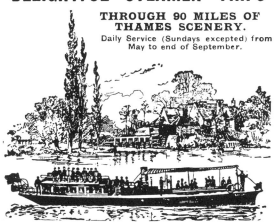

DELIGHTFUL STEAMER TRIPS

THROUGH 90 MILES OF THAMES SCENERY.

Daily Service (Sundays excepted) from
May to end of September.

SALOON STEAMERS run daily (Sundays excepted)
between **OXFORD, HENLEY, & KINGSTON.**

DOWN TRIP.		UP TRIP.	
Oxford dep.	9.30 a.m., 2.30 p.m.	Kingston dep.	9.0 a.m., 2.30 p.m.
Wallingford arr. abt.	1.40 p.m., 6.40 p.m.	Windsor arr. about	1.40 p.m., 7.15 p.m.
„ dep. abt.	2.40 p.m., 9.0 a.m.	„ dep.	2.40 p.m., 9.15 a.m.
Henley arr. about	7.0 p.m., 1.30 p.m.	Henley arr. „	7.15 p.m., 1.40 p.m.
„ dep. „	9.50 a.m., 2.40 p.m.	„ dep.	9.0 a.m., 2.40 p.m.
Windsor arr. „	1.45 p.m., 7.15 p.m.	Wallingford arr. „	1.40 p.m., 7.15 p.m.
„ dep. „	2.40 p.m., 9.15 a.m.	„ dep. „	2.40 p.m., 9.0 a.m.
Kingston arr. „	7.10 p.m., 1.30 p.m.	Oxford arr. „	7.10 p.m., 1.15 p.m.

The through journey occupies two days each way, but passengers can join or leave the
boat at any of the locks or regular stopping places. Circular Tickets for combined Railway and Steamer Trips are issued at most of the principal G.W.R. Stations, also at
Waterloo, Richmond, and Kingston Stations, L. & S.W. Railway. Time Tables giving
full particulars of arrangements, fares, etc., post free, **1d.**

ROWING BOATS of all kinds for Excursions down the River at
Charges which include Cartage back to Oxford.
Full Particulars on application.

STEAM, ELECTRIC AND MOTOR LAUNCHES for Hire by the
Day or Week, and also for the Trip.

Boats of every description, Canoes, Punts, &c., built to order
A large selection, both New & Second-hand, kept in readiness for Sale or Hire.
Illustrated Price Lists may be had on application.
HOUSE BOATS FOR SALE OR HIRE, & ALSO BUILT TO ORDER.

SALTER BROTHERS, Boat Builders, Folly Bridge, OXFORD.

By the mid-20th century the river was used more for recreation than trade. This 1914 advertisement not only shows a saloon steamer run by Salter Brothers of Folly Bridge, which took two days each way to travel from Oxford to Kingston, but also advertises steam, electric and motor launches for hire by the day or week. The picture still shows Iffley Water Mill which had been destroyed by fire six years earlier. It was also possible, in the early years of the 20th century, to travel by horse-drawn houseboat to Nuneham Courtenay.

Looking downstream from Iffley. The date is unknown. The Isis on the Oxford side of Iffley has been associated with the sport of rowing for generations. The colleges of the University have competed against each other twice a year for 150 years. From about 1825 until about 1839, crews raced from Iffley lock itself, starting when the lock gates were opened. The bumping races began when there were too many crews to begin from the lock. By 1849 20 eights took part in the summer races. The river, being too narrow for crews to row side by side, the object is to bump the boat in front and thus take their position in the rowing order.

The Queen's College Torpids crew being polled off the start in 1913. Torpids (once known as 'Toggers') are rowed in the Hilary (winter) term and Eights in the Trinity (summer) term.

St Peter's College women's Torpids crew about to row off in 1999. They were top of one division and were starting bottom of the next division up.

Until the mid-20th century the college barges added attraction to the scene. Now they have been replaced by more mundane boat houses on the bank. The top photograph shows rowing men carrying their oars during Eights Week of 1920. Second from the left is Pat Mallam (later a well-respected Oxford medical man). He gained his rowing blue for the University. The centre photograph shows a Torpids crew in 1920 and the bottom picture a scene between races at Eights the same year.

In 1842 the City of Oxford Regatta moved to a reach between Oxford and Iffley and by 1860 it had become the Royal Regatta. Iffley once had its own rowing club which used to enter the City races. It was called the Iffley Twisters. The Riverside Club at Donnington bridge was opened in 1964 to provide facilities for rowing clubs. The bridge was built at a cost of £248,000 and was officially opened by Lord Hailsham, one-time Member of Parliament for Oxford, in 1962. It links the Abingdon and Iffley Roads.

'Poplars, twin sisters, whispering side by side
The winds unite them and the winds divide.'

George Santayana

On the left is the lock-keeper's house and on the right the weir. The island's poplars died off but are remembered as surviving up to the 1960s by people who were living in Iffley at the time. (Courtesy *Oxford Mail and Times*)

The river near the lock in the early years of the 19th century. The Manor House is in the background. (Courtesy Miss Betty Mayall)

The weir in snow, 1990.

Iffley Lock in July, 1968 (courtesy *Oxford Mail and Times*). The lock garden, kept then by Mr L C Farley, tied for second position in the Thames Conservancy competition for 1968. The lock-keeper was Mr. R A Wright.

The lock and lock-keeper's house with visiting geese in February, 1999.

The first lock was built in 1632 and was one of the first pound locks on the Thames. It was rebuilt in 1774. The present lock was built in 1924. Custom had it that if a dead body was carried over the lock it would create a right of way. Corpses from the opposite bank had therefore to be taken round by boat on the way to the Church. As recently as 1948 the toll-keeper refused permission to police to pass over the toll-bridge with the body of a drowned man. The lock was owned by Lincoln College and tolls were extracted from the pockets of pedestrians and paid to the college.

The Tolls

Phil Surman, in her book *Pride of the Morning* (Alan Sutton, 1992) tells of the time when no one was supposed to pass the toll-house, at the end of the second bridge, without paying their halfpenny (or penny return). She writes: 'The toll was unpopular among the residents, some of whom would march past the outstretched hand of the toll-gate keeper with the one word 'Iffley" as though it were a magic password. Surman recalls the day when some American tourists protested and when they asked what was done with the money, the keeper replied: 'We give it away in prizes to people who mind their own business.'

It is said that when Edward VII (at that time Prince of Wales) was walking past the toll-gate, an old woman, whose duty it was to collect the tolls and who sat there from 8 a,m. to 8 p.m., shouted at him to come back and pay his money. When his aide de campe, who was walking behind the Prince, asked 'But don't you know who he is?' the reply was 'I don't care if 'ese the King of England but 'ese got to pay 'is 'alfpenny just the same.'

Mr Bert Cunnington collecting a toll from a lady in December, 1939. Bert, whose father was the village carpenter and made the coffins, lived in a cottage at the top of the lane which had a gate giving access to the path to the toll-gate. Bert, who wore rubber boots because of his painful corns, smoothed out that part of the path which he needed to traverse. His job at the toll-gate, which included selling ice cream, sweets and cigarettes on behalf of the village shop, was Bert's whole life. He started there in the 1920s and only stopped when the tolls ceased. Harry Thompson, who worked as a gardener at Court Place, was his great friend and they would sit together at the toll-gate for hours, not always agreeing about things.

By 1956 negotiations started between Oxford City Council and Lincoln College, in an attempt to end the system but although there were periods after that when the tolls ceased to be collected it seems that they continued on and off until at least 1961. In the autumn of that year Mrs Rouse, wife of the lock-keeper, told an *Oxford Times* reporter that she had put up a sign on the closed and shuttered toll-gate keeper's hut which read 'TOLL 1 penny please ', indicating a slit for letters. Mrs Rouse still had to pay rent for collecting the toll to Lincoln College. The Rouses kept a small shop nearby. (Courtesy *Oxford Mail and Times*)

Mr Christopher Robin Alden outside his shop at Iffley Lock in February, 1999.

The Roving Bridge (now more commonly known as Desborough Bridge) with balustrades on either side, is listed Grade II of special architectural or historical interest. It is early 19th century. On the landing is a bronze bull's or ox's head, modelled on Red Michael, a prize bull in Lord Desborough's herd. There is also a starting ring which is inscribed OUBC (Oxford University Boat Club) 1924, the date the new lock was opened. Desborough, a former President of OUBC, was anxious that the Blues' boat should be first through the new lock. The bridge is 20 metres upstream from Iffley lock. The photograph was taken in February, 1999.

The Water Mill

The mill was a favourite subject for artists of which this is an early 19th century example. It is not mentioned in Domesday (1086) but in the late 12th century it is recorded that Juliana de Remy gave 18 pence rent from the mill to each of the nearby hospitals, St Bartholomew's and St John's. The mill, which was used for grinding corn, was purchased by Lincoln College in 1445.

Another artist's impression of Iffley mill. This is from an etching by A Branet-Debaines, probably undertaken in about 1845.

A photograph of the mill and weir taken in about 1895, courtesy of Iffley Church. Throughout much of the 19th century, until about 1890, the mill had been under threat because of plans to pull down the lock and weirs when it was thought that they were the cause of flooding of the low-lying areas closer to Oxford. If this plan had been carried out the mill would have lost its water power. Pressure for something to be done about the epidemics and diseases caused by this flooding came from Sir Henry Acland, the well-known physician of the time, Dean Liddell of Christ Church, who was Vice-Chancellor 1870–74, and later from Sir Benjamin Jowett, Master of Balliol, Vice-Chancellor, 1882–1886. In the end no work was carried out and Iffley lock remained in existence.

From 1890 to 1908 the lessee of the mill, Mr Joe Wilson, lived in the adjoining house but leased the mill to the Iffley baker, Mr Jackman, who used it for grinding. His bakery was at the corner of Baker's lane but it is no longer there. (See the Tree Hotel, Section 8).

A photograph taken by Henry Taunt showing the position of the mill in relation to the lock in 1855. (Copyright Jeremy's Reproduction Postcards, Oxford Stamp Centre). Henry Taunt, in his account of Iffley mill, described it as 'solidly built of stone, its antiquated walls have stood the storms and floods of over seven hundred years'.

The mill in winter in the late 19th century taken by George Washington Wilson, a professional photographer of the day. (Courtesy *Oxford Mail and Times*)

Having survived the threat to its existence through much of the 19th century, the mill was destroyed by a disastrous fire in the early evening of 20th May, 1908. According to a report in *The Oxford Times* of 23rd May, three days after the fire, the alarm was given at about 6.30 p.m. by a man who had just paid his toll at the gate and was about to cross the river. The mill was full of grain at the time and the possible cause was overheating. It was fortunate that it did not occur at night when people would have been sleeping above the grinding room. The Mill House was also affected and the mill-owner's wife, who was an invalid, was able to be rescued, as was a quantity of furniture.

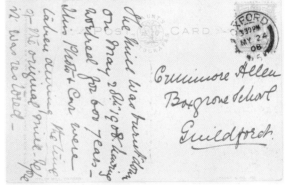

A postcard addressed to the young Cullimore Allen (see Section 10) who was away at school. It is dated 24th May, explaining that the fire at the mill took place four days before. (Courtesy Mrs V Allen)

Unfortunately, the mill was not insured at the time, it having lasped when Mr Wilson (see Section 10, Wilsons and Wyatts) had sub-let it. The fire must have been a spectacular sight and could be seen from the railway line. It was seen by the miller who was returning by train to Oxford, having atttended an agricultural show, but he arrived too late to do anything about it.

A leader in *The Oxford Times* of 23rd May stated that the destruction of the mill 'will be deeply regretted by the hundreds of artists and votaries of the camera who were never tired of the endeavour to place the mill and its surroundings on canvas or paper in some new light or from some new point of vantage.'

A photograph taken the day after the fire showing the mill destroyed. (Copyright Oxford Stamp Centre)

Numerous sightseers came to view the devastation. Mrs Violet Webb, who was just two years old at the time, can remember the occasion as if it were yesterday. She says that the village was swarming with people on foot, bicycles, ponies and traps and cars. Note the baby in the pram on the left. Sightseers outnumbered villagers and some of the latter, returning home on the evening of the fire, could not imagine what was the cause of the crowds.

The ruins of Iffley mill after the fire on 20th May, 1908. (Courtesy of Iffley Church)

Grist Cottage and two surviving grind-stones which are the last remnants of Iffley water mill. Photograph taken in 1999. The mill was never rebuilt.

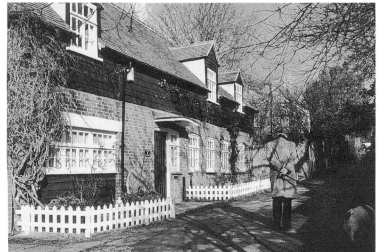

In the vicinity of the site of the old mill, some Iffley residents enjoying a river outing near the steps of a garden. (Courtesy Mrs Joyce Marchant)

A scholarly history of the mill has been written by Mr John Perrott. Called *Iffley Water Mill*, it is a publication of the Iffley Local History Society and can be obtained locally

Schools

The Nowells

Sarah Munday, the daughter of a rich Oxford tradesman who had been Mayor in 1760/61, married the Reverend Thomas Nowell at St Aldate's Church in February, 1764. He was the new Principal of St Mary Hall which later became part of Oriel College. Sarah's father, by virtue of his being Mayor at the time of the coronation of George III, took on the traditional position of one of the two Chief Butlers of England for the ceremony and handed the King a glass of wine on the day. For undertaking this duty he was knighted and became Sir Thomas Munday. His upholstery business was so successful that his daughter received a handsome fortune. In 1771, Nowell became Regius Professor of Modern History at Oxford University.

A few years after their marriage, the prosperous Nowells came to Iffley and lived at the Manor House (see Section 1). Sadly, their only child, a boy, died in infancy. Here, then, was the childless Sarah with time on her hands and who probably inherited some of her father's interest in public and charitable work. At first she paid for some of the village children to be taught to read and sew. She was following in the tradition of Alice Smith who had set up the first Iffley charity and on which, by coincidence, Sir Thomas Munday had once been a trustee, a position which Thomas Nowell later held.

Sarah obviously wished to do more than pay for a few classes and in due course to employ a schoolmistress, provide a place in which to have the classes, and to provide clothing as well as education for some of the poorer children. It was by Sarah's will — she died in 1800 and Thomas died in 1801 — that the Alice Smith charity was to receive the money in order to set up the school. The will went into some detail about what the trustees should do. They were to see that eight poor girls and two poor boys from Iffley, between the ages of six and twelve, should attend. Even the style of dress for the children was laid down and the girls' wear was to include a straw hat with a green ribbon and the boys a shirt and strong shoes. However, because of a problem with the terms of the will, it was not until the time of Margaret Nowell, Sarah and Thomas's niece, that the school actually began in 1805. At first classes took place in the cottage of Hannah Cripps, the first schoolmistress, who was the wife of the parish clerk. The salary of the mistress was always paid by the charity up to the time the school closed.

The school (see photograph on following page) was eventually built, the inscription on the plaque reading: 'Sarah Nowell's School 1822.' As Sarah Nowell had intended, the Nowell scholars were both clothed and educated. The girls were provided with red flannel cloaks and bonnets and with dresses in summer. The local historian, Edward Cordrey remembered seeing the Nowell scholars coming to Matins in Iffley Church in their bright red cloaks each Sunday. They had to stay 'to endure the sermon while the younger ones were mercifully let out beforehand.' The scholars were educated without

Nowell's School taken in 1990.

payment until they were 12 years of age when, if they stayed, they had to pay threepence a week.

In due course the house became, over the years, the residence of head masters or head mistresses of the Parochial School until, in 1885 it was rented out. The Polley family (see Section 10) lived there from 1902 to 1985. Mrs Violet Webb, née Polley, who with her husband rented Nowell House after her parents had done so, tells me that Nowell House had a ghost. On a foggy November night the back door opened and it was thought that young Mr Polley had come in. This happened three times but no one was there. One morning they heard someone walking upstairs and, on investigation, the figure looked like one of the little girl pupils. Someone also once saw her in a school cloak on the lawn. This was long after the house was a school.

In 1853 the school amalgamated with the Parish School which had been taking Nowell scholars for some classes since its inception. The school house was sold by auction in 1985 by the Trustees of the Sarah Nowell's Educational Foundation and it is now in private ownership.

A full history of the School, including an account of the original charity papers, may be found in *Sarah Nowell's School. Charity at Work in Old Iffley,* by S K Fairfield, published in June, 1988, privately printed and sold on behalf of Iffley Church Hall.

Iffley Parochial School

Iffley Parochial School, as the inscription on the opposite page indicates, was started in 1838 in this large converted barn in Church Way. In due course Sarah Nowell scholars and the children of widows were admitted free. The benefaction of Sarah Nowell helped to pay some of the expenses of the school and for 15 Nowell scholars until times

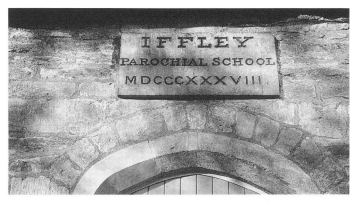

changed and there was free education for all. The charity income then went to assist children in need of financial help. The infant school was established in 1854.

Fortunately, records exist about life as a child at this school in the latter part of the 19th century. Edward Cordrey gave an account of his schooldays on the occasion of the closure of the school in December, 1961. From a family of 13 children, nine siblings had preceded him at the school and three followed. In the parish magazine of January, 1962 Cordrey recalls the dark and dismal interior with the windows facing Church Way bricked up. They never saw flowers, plants or pictures as in today's schools. He wrote: 'The chief ornament fixed in my memory was the cane.' It was frequently used by Mr Wilson, the headmaster. The girls, under Mrs Mason's tuition, were well known for their needlework and took most of the prizes in the Oxfordshire Schools Needlework Competition held in Oxford Town Hall. The Nowell scholars, both boys and girls, had to knit their own stockings and help make their own clothes with materials provided. Queen Victoria's Diamond Jubilee was a memorable occasion when there was a river trip to Nuneham Courtenay for the whole school in a house-boat drawn by two horses and there was a band and a Punch and Judy show on board.

Violet Webb, née Polley, was born in 1906 and clearly remembers going to school here at the age of three. She recalls her first day there when she was frightened that the blackboard would fall on her. Having been given an apple to take to school, she did not know what she was supposed to do with it and held it in her hand all day. Dolly Ward (née Bull), who was born in 1916, had a much more traumatic experience because on her first day she did not stay long and ran all the way home. However, the next day she returned and enjoyed school ever afterwards.

Church Way, Iffley in 1960. (Courtesy of Iffley Church) Note the school sign this side of the school. The building was once a medieval barn, smithy and wheelwright shop. The house on the left is No. 122, originally known as Court House, a listed Grade II building. The school remained a church school under the City of Oxford Education department until it closed on St Thomas's day, 21st December, 1961, ending 123 years of history.

There was a carol service in the Church which was lit by candles; the children were each given a bound copy of The Bible and the teachers received cheques. The children then attended either Rose Hill or Donnington schools.

The old school building is now the Church Hall. Photograph taken in 1999.

Iffley Mead School

The school was opened at Iffley Turn in September, 1969, having been built the previous spring. It is a school for moderate learning and provides education for temporary periods or throughout their school life for 5–16 year olds.

The new gym at Iffley Mead in 1969.

Sports Day at Iffley Mead in 1971. Watching the children competing in a sack race are (left) Miss Jane Hudson, classroom teacher, and (right) Miss Pauline Parriss (P.E.) who, now Mrs Harris, still teaches at the school.

In January, 1976 the school suffered a disastrous fire. *The Oxford Mail* reported that it was in ruins after the big blaze. 'About 180 Oxfordshire children with learning difficulties,' they reported, 'will not be starting school as planned tomorrow after a fire during the night of 11 January destroyed more than half of the school.' The alarm was raised at 10.45 p.m. by Robert Huntley who happened to be staying with his mother at 4 Hartley Russell Close. The Headmaster, Mr Charles Brees, said about this devastating blow that he was 'shocked and shattered' by what he saw. Arrangements were made for the pupils to go to two other schools while Iffley Mead was rebuilt. By May some of the children were able to return to new classrooms. When, in October, 1977 the brand new school was ready it was said: 'It's marvellous what can come out of adversity.' Help had come in from all over Oxford.

Iffley Mead children playing shop at the school in the late 1970s.

In 1999, Mr John Knox, Head of Iffley Mead, completed 25 years in the post. The 111 children in school that year came from all over Oxfordshire.

St Augustine's School

This Roman Catholic/Church of England Upper School is situated at Iffley Turn next door to Iffley Mead.

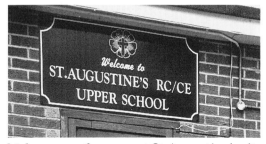

In 1984 St Edmund Campion R.C. School, which was on the present St Augustine's site, and Cowley St John Upper School were united to cater for Anglicans, Roman Catholics and children of other denominations in the City of Oxford and surrounding areas. For two years it operated on split sites and then, in 1986, after the addition of new, purpose-built facilities, was established at Iffley Turn with the name of St Augustine of Canterbury. The name was chosen because it was Augustine who had been sent from

Rome to convert the English and became the first Archbishop of Canterbury. He is therefore a patron of both the Anglican and Roman Catholic churches. The school is well-equipped with a wide range of specialist rooms, including a chapel, drama studio, seven science laboratories and a careers centre which is based in the library.

The mural, with gold lettering on a dark blue background, is in the entrance hall of the school. It was painted by Dawn Parsonage as her A level design project. She is seated in front.

Above: St Augustine's has an excellent academic record. Here Regina Lally and her younger brother John are celebrating their good A Level (GCSE) results in August, 1997. She was at Exeter University in 1999.

Right: Margaret Griffin opening her GCSE results in August, 1998. She went on to Cambridge University from St Augustine's.

In February, 1999 St Augustine's had an excellent Office for Standards in Education (OFSTED) report which commented on good calibre staff, good teaching and a very positive atmosphere and effective sixth form. It was reported that students behaved well and that there were good relationships between all members of the school. GCSE results were above average.

In January, 1998 the under-16 football team was one of the top 64 schools in the country.

Fourteen languages are spoken at the school: Spanish, Cantonese, Tamil, Ki-Swahili (Uganda), Bengali, Malay, German, French, Hindi, English, Punjabi, Urdu, Italian and Gujarati.

A group of St Augustine's students and the Head Teacher, Mrs Elizabeth Gilpin, in the front of the school in March, 1999. The stone figure of St Augustine can be seen on the wall, top right.

An experiment in one of the laboratories at St Augustine's. Left to right: Mathew Cothier, Laura Teeling, Natalie Moore, Bridgitte McGlynn, and Kathryn Allsworth.

Pupils and their Head Teacher at St Augustine's. Left to right, back row: Christopher Williams, James Sheppard, Paul Middleton, Craig Fenemore. Front row: Clodagh Murphy, Katie Daniel, Mrs. Gilpin, Kaleigh Johnson, Donna Hammond.

The same students in a more informal pose. Left to right: Paul Middleton, Clodagh Murphy, Katie Daniel, Craig Fenemore, Kaleigh Johnson, Donna Hammond, James Sheppard, Christopher Williams.

May Day

*'While the maidens in array
Crown the Happy Queen of May.'*

For many years May Day was an important event in the Iffley calendar. The traditional May Day songs, sung unaccompanied, were handed down from older to younger children, practised for weeks beforehand and learnt by heart.

The children had a holiday from school and activities included a church service, a procession and collecting money from houses in the village. It was, of course, an honour to be elected by one's school-fellows as Queen or King of the May but there were other positions to be filled such as maids of honour, escorts, junior policemen, treasurers, garlanders, guards and macebearers, the whole court often numbering as many as 40 children. The girls wore starched dresses and flowers in their hats. Fritillaries, found in profusion in Iffley's meadows, often formed a major part of the garlands.

In most years, at the end of the day a well-earned tea was held back at school, the cost of which was met from the contents of the collecting boxes which were usually covered with leaves and flowers.

May Day at the turn of the century. That year Phyllis Ludlow was Queen of the May. To the left, between her escort and a young policeman carrying a garlanded pole, is Annie Polley. To the right of Annie is Harry Polley, also with a garlanded stave. (Copyright Oxford Stamp Centre).

Children practising their songs in 1951. (Courtesy Mrs Linda Youthed).

May Day procession in 1956. The May Queen is Pat Beesley and her escort (centre right) was Ernest Horwood. The procession here is made up of the top class of the school. In the traditional way the boys carry poles wreathed with flowers and the girls have garlands in their hair. On arrival at the Church the Vicar conducted a short service. (Courtesy *Oxford Mail and Times*)

May Day in 1959. The procession, headed by the May Queen and King, is starting off from the school. (Courtesy *Oxford Mail and Times*)

Donnington Junior School children dancing at Iffley in May, 1964. After Iffley school closed in 1961 many of the children attended Donnington. In the background, standing between the Rectory and the Church, can be seen the Reverend Jonathan Hills with Mrs Otto, mother of one of the girls taking part in the dancing. Seated in front of the Rectory door, on a chair, wearing a hat, is thought to be Miss Evelyn Banks. She lived at Malthouse Cottage and was an authority on the life and history of the village. She played a major part in the compilation of the Iffley W.I. prizewinning Scrap Book of 1955. Second from Miss Banks (on the right) is Mrs Cumber. (Courtesy of *Oxford Mail and Times*).

May Day celebrations outside the Church in 1967. Teachers are standing at the rear. (Courtesy of Mr Ron Bromley)

At one time when there were also Mummers' plays performed, traditional Iffley songs were sung at Christmas as well as on May Day but these died out long ago according to Dr G D Parkes and Mary Parkes in their book *May Day in Iffley*. This book not only included the history of the event but recorded for posterity the May Day songs before they too were forgotten. The book was privately published and circulated in 1934, just at the time when children over the age of 11 no longer attended the village school. Dr Parkes and his wife Mary lived at Broomfield on Rose Hill.

The ancient Order of Foresters Friendly Society also processed on their Feast Day in early July, young and old members assembling at The Tree in their Sunday best. They wore huge buttonholes, the regalia of their order and sashes of brilliant green and red silk often trimmed with sequins. Boys carried wooden swords and clubs. The great banner was carried aloft and when they reached Iffley Turn they were met by a country band, finally ending up at the Church. A dinner at The Tree was held in a large marquee. A fair was held on Foresters' Day in the little field behind The Tree and a half-day was taken off school. There was dancing, often to the tune of 'See me dance the polka' and festivities continued until 10 p.m. Another fair was usually held in September. These activities continued well into the 20th century. The Secretary of the Iffley Foresters' Court, Hearts of Oak, Mr T H Morris, was still recorded in Kelly's Directory in 1949. The Friendly Society movement ran insurance schemes, providing benefits in case of sickness, infirmity or death and based themselves on a mixture of ritual and benevolence.

The Community

The Memorial Institute

A hall to commemorate the men of Iffley who lost their lives in the First World War was given to the village by Sir George Forrest and housed in an annexe to The Five Bells public house which used to stand on the west side of Church Way.

The first Institute was later replaced by this green, corrugated iron building. As well as being the home of many social events, the Iffley Women's Institute met here for 40 years until the building fell into disrepair and was demolished by the Donnington Trust in 1973.

The cottage which adjoined the above in which lived the caretakers of the Memorial Hall, Mr and Mrs Baker. They served loyally for 33 years. The house was demolished in October, 1969.

As in most villages during the Second World War, there was an enhanced community spirit. In Iffley, which was already a friendly place in which to live, people came together to help the war effort. A Red Cross Sale was held during the early years of the war to help raise funds. In this photograph can be seen (in front) the garden strips in which members of the Iffley Children's Gardening Club grew vegetables. Each had a plot and the produce was sold. The Club also performed plays, one being *Snow White and the Seven Dwarfs* set to music. This was in aid of the Red Cross and the Prisoners of War Fund. (Photograph courtesy of Mr Ron Bromley). Back row (left to right): Mrs Sylvester, Squadron-Leader York Bramble, Mrs Maud A M White (Councillor for Cowley and Iffley Ward, 1934–1947 who was Mayor in 1942), Lord Slessor, Miss Wall, Alice Knight, Mary Fisher, Mrs Rutherford. Middle row: Derek Ives, Mrs Ives (behind), Joan Fisher-Ridden, Mrs Hawkins, Mrs Stretton, Mrs Coles, Mrs Cripps with Hazel Cripps, baby Harley with Mrs Harley, Lady Slessor, Mrs Bretheston. Front row: Brian Sylvester, John Cripps, Margaret Ives, Audrey Stretton, Freda Rutherford, Daphne Coles, Betty Beasley, Royce Coles, Bill Rutherford.

During the war the Memorial Hall was used as a clearing house for children evacuated from vulnerable cities. There were, of course, Air Raid Wardens (see Section 2) and on one occasion a member of the Home Guard, hearing a suspicious rustling in a hedge at night is reputed to have shot a hedgehog. Permits were available to obtain sugar for jam making and Mrs Marchant's kitchen (see Section 10) was used for this purpose. A preserving centre was opened and fruit trees were bought and planted which provided the ingredients for the jam. Seeds were received from Canada and the USA. In 1941, 280 pounds of jam were made and sold at Messrs Grimbley Hughes, the well-known provision merchants in Oxford's Cornmarket. Also, many pounds of chutney and pickles were made by the W.I. and sold to fellow members. A member of the Headington Quarry W.I. came to Iffley to encourage Institute members to keep goats, rabbits and chickens and to provide extra vegetables and fruit (see Section 8).

As was the case in every community in Britain, there were celebrations when the war was over in Europe in May, 1945. This photograph, courtesy of Mr Ron Bromley, was taken on V.E. Day in Church Way in front of Nowell House. Back row (left to right): Mrs Fisher (on edge of picture), Mrs Webb, Mrs Schoon, Mrs Polley (see Section 10), who lived at Nowell House, Mrs Rutherford, Miss Schoon (in hat), Miss Harley (holding a baby), Mrs Coles, Miss Josephine Beesley (back to camera), Miss Nellie Cumber, Mrs Cripps. Middle row: Margaret Ives, facing camera and eating, Graham Webb, William Rutherford, John Cripps, –, –, –, Joyce Derbyshire, Freda Rutherford, Pauline Crawford (big bow in hair). In front: Ann Stretton, Hazel Cripps (with doll).

The Iffley Tapestry. On the wall of the Church Hall is displayed the magnificent tapestry which records the history of the village from 1170 to 1987. Seen with it here, before it was hung, is (left) Mrs Cynthia Low and Mrs Bronwen Huntley. With Mrs Debbie Brown and Miss Sheila Fairfield, they were the driving force behind the project. The idea came from Mrs Huntley who saw a similar tapestry on a visit to the New Forest which had been put together by 52 people. It is made up of 52 six-inch square sections mainly depicting views and symbols of Iffley. There were no sponsors and it was the work of 32 needlewomen and artists. Not one square was refused. Wool was provided by the organisers (on payment of £1) which meant that it was all made of the same material. It was a joyful year's work with not one disagreement on the committee. The 'rose window' in the centre is made up of 12 triangles which depict the birds and flowers of the village. (Copyright *Oxford Mail and Times.*)

The Glebe.

This field gives a necessary and attractive breathing space at the southern end of the village on the east side of Church Way. In fact, it could be said that it is one of the main features which help Iffley to retain its village character. It is just north of the church and opposite the Church Hall and the original Court House (now 122 Church Way). It was under a serious threat in about 1991 when the Diocese applied for planning permission to develop it for housing. The Friends of Iffley (see below), under the chairmanship of Mr Stan Garrod, went into action immediately. In the end there was so much opposition to the plans that they were not proceeded with. To make sure that the Glebe would never be developed there was an offer to buy it. As a plaque in the Church Hall now records: *The Glebe Field was purchased on 29th October, 1996 from the Diocese of Oxford by the Oxford Preservation Trust with a donation given by John and Joan Critchley* (see Section 10) *to mark 50 years in Iffley*. The decision to involve the Preservation Trust (of which Mr John Critchley was a Trustee) was so that they could take on the land holding and maintain the field in perpetuity, thus ensuring that the rural nature of that part of the village remained.

The Friends of Iffley Village

The first committee meeting was elected on 2nd December, 1959 as a response to some of the threats to the environment of the village. It is still an important part of Iffley life and is always alert to any unsuitable building developments.

An early issue was that of Denton House which it was hoped to prevent being converted into offices for the Water department of Oxford City Council. A petition with 157 signatures was unsuccessful but the Friends learnt a lot from the campaign, especially about the workings of the local authority and the attitude of its members.

The Friends from time to time make sure that the posts which stand at the eastern entrance to Tree Lane are retained. From the beginning the Friends maintained that the posts were important to Iffley because they were what 'keeps it a village'. Another early issue – and one which has run and run – is the question of tipping rubbish on the water meadows. The Friends wish to ensure that as many fields as possible can be retained as they have been 'immemorially' with all their flora and fauna. The meadows are grazed by sheep and visited by water-fowl.

There is also a record of another issue which came up when the Friends had not been established long, a complaint about 'the squalid approach to the toll-gate' which read: 'There is much in Iffley to delight the eye but little by little it is being whittled away and replaced by what is known as 'subtopia''. In 1993, in consultation with the Friends, the City Council agreed to replace modern lighting with 18th century-type lanterns. The protection of the trees of the village is another important item of importance to the Friends.

An evening party of the Friends of Iffley in the Church Hall on 6th February, 1999. Welcoming members and friends is Sir John Elliot, FBA, Regius Professor of Modern History at Oxford University 1990–97, who chairs the Friends. He is a Fellow of Oriel College, has written many books and received a considerable number of prizes and honours. In the year this party was held the membership of the Friends stood at nearly 400.

In the photograph can also be seen Geoff Schofield, Elizabeth and John Leigh, Liz Julier, Professor Denis Nineham (former Warden of Keble College) and, seated to the rear under the archway, Dr Charlotte Banks, who is an honorary life member. Her aunt was also prominent in village life (see Section 6). Seated on the right is Rob Liebermann (Planning Chairman of the Friends) and, standing, Peter Rogers (Hon. Treasurer).

Helpers at the Friends of Iffley party in February, 1999. Left to right: Anne Ryan, Thelma Bennett, Lydia Penwarden.

Members of the Friends at their 1999 February party. They are listening to Professor Ryan who is playing tunes connected with Iffley on the piano. Left to right; Betty Mayall, John Critchley, Andrew Cuneo (visitor), the Reverend Michael Lea (Vicar of Iffley).

Mrs Graham Greene and Margaret Brown talking to a visitor, Andrew Cuneo.

The Iffley Local History Society

The Society, which was begun in 1964, has well-attended meetings and a membership of between 60 and 70. They collect archives of the village and publish booklets on the history of Iffley.

The Chairman of Iffley Local History Society, Mr John Perrott, speaking to Mrs Joanna Mathews at the April, 1999 meeting of the Society in the Church Hall. Note the Iffley tapestry on the wall behind.

Iffley Women's Institute

Founded in October, 1923, the Institute survived a threatened closure in 1929 and celebrated its 75th anniversary before closing in 1998. Its Founder and first President was Miss E Sing and Miss E Phelps was President from 1929 until 1944.

For many years, until it was demolished in 1973, the Institute met at the Memorial Hall (See Section 7). One older member recalled that during the first few years 'we sat on a square of red carpet and in winter all huddled round a stove half-way down the hall.' Miss Phelps, President, would for the Christmas meeting dress in a full-length flowing red gown with a high boned collar. 'She seemed like the Queen of Iffley' and members 'almost gave a bob' as she came in.

Drama was a favourite activity and this shows members of the Institute who took part in the W.I. Pageant of 1926 in Worcester College gardens.

The choir was also popular from the early days of the Institute. Once, (probably in the 1920s) Miss Imogen Holst, (the daughter of the composer Gustav Holst), who was living for a time in Iffley, conducted the Institute's Christmas carols. Imogen, who lived

from 1907 to 1984, was a distinguished musician, scholar, teacher and writer about music and was awarded the CBE in 1975.

The photograph shows the Institute's Choral Society which was formed in 1937 and flourished right up to the 1950s. They performed in festivals in Oxford. The choir was for a time conducted by Dr G D Parkes (see Section 6). Male voices were added and it then became the Iffley Choral Society. Other activities included cookery demonstrations and in the early years were given by Miss Petty at 'Rivermead'. Known as the 'Pudding Lady', she tried to convince W.I. members that the water in which green vegetables were cooked should never be thrown away as it was beneficial to health, especially as a cure for rheumatism. When they were sceptical the Pudding Lady threatened to haunt them if they did not take her advice.

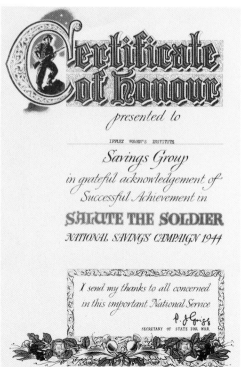

The Institute's certificate of honour given for their National Savings efforts in the Second World War. Members did much in wartime to utilise their skills to add to meagre rations. When there was clothes rationing Mrs Mary Parkes taught members how to make slippers out of the felt and velour of old hats. It was said that it was not safe to leave one's hat lying around.

The cover of the prize-winning Scrap Book of 1955. Fifty entries were received from all over the County for the competition which was organised by Oxfordshire Rural Community Council. The book was the work of Miss M Evelyn Banks (President of the Institute from 1952 to 1955) with Miss Anne James and the assistance of many helpers. It won the first prize of £25. It is a unique and valuable record of the life of the village. Although reflecting a different approach from that of the professional historians, it was well-researched and illustrated in detail. The cover was designed by Mr Kiewe of Ship Street, Oxford, the embroidery expert, and the handwork was mainly the work of Mrs I Crisp. Note the fritillaries which are still to be found in Iffley meadows. The book is now in the Centre for Oxfordshire Studies.

A Fête run by Iffley W.I. outside the Memorial Hall on 15th May, 1965, which was opened by Dr Kathleen Warin (seen on the left picking out a tombola ticket). In the centre is Mrs C Powell and on the right are Mrs L Jeffs (partly hidden), Mrs G Hudson, Mrs I Crisp (holding box) and Mrs A Thomas.

(All Women's Institute photographs courtesy of Mrs. I Crisp.)

Shops, Hotels and Public Houses

The Old Store was situated opposite the Prince of Wales public house and is now a private home. Mr Goodwin was the proprietor of the store for many years. He is seen here (right) with Mr Tom Collis (see Section 3) who kindly lent the photograph. The date is not known.

In the old days there were many shops and trades. In 1852, for instance, there was a butcher (Mr John French), two bakers (Mr John Haynes and Mr John White), a grocer (Mr John Collett), a coal merchant and many more traders. Before gas was laid on, the custom was to take dinner to the bakers on Sundays. The cost charged by the baker for cooking one's pie was one penny but to cook a whole joint and potatoes cost 1½ pence.

Obviously the shopkeepers were glad of village custom and the stores were particularly well patronised. There was apparently an intelligent maiden lady called Norah Grayson who lived at 'Lucia' after the Second World War. She sometimes bicycled 30 miles a day when she worked in Reading. Once she cycled into Oxford and bought a cake and the news of this somehow reached the baker. When she next went to him to buy her bread it is said that he told her: 'You will buy your bread where you buy your cake' and would not serve her.

Mr Bill Gibbs and his wife Nina who owned the post office and general store until 1967. The Clinic replaced the store. Note the large jars of sweets in the window. Tunbridge and Dicks owned the store before the Gibbs came to Iffley in May, 1954. The change-over coincided with the time when the last item of food came off the ration after the war (this was fats including butter.) Mr Goodwin had always been at loggerheads with the Gibbs' predecessors but Mr Gibbs tactfully suggested that the past should be forgotten and a friendship developed between them. Mr Goodwin would even come into Mr Gibbs' shop to rasher his bacon. The Gibbs had a son and daughter, Michael and Rosmund [sic].

The business included that at the toll-gate until it ended. The Gibbs were a mine of information for all newcomers to the village. On one occasion when there was a fire at a house in Tree Lane the occupants had to go into a hotel. Mr Gibbs was asked to look after their cat who promptly produced kittens. Before the shops were built at Rose Hill the business supplied the whole of Rose Hill as well as Iffley. The first week Bill and Nina Gibbs arrived in Iffley they saw the farmer's son driving a large pig along Church Way to the piggery near Court Place. They felt that they had really arrrived in the country. (Information and photograph courtesy Mr Bill Gibbs.)

Morella's shop next to the Prince of Wales' public house in Church Way. Also a post office, this was closed in May, 1999. A group of Iffley volunteers, with financial support from the Friends of Iffley, now runs the shop and post-office which was officially opened by the Lord Mayor on 25th October, 1999.

The Tree Hotel

Now a welcoming, family-run hotel on the corner of Church and Tree Lane, its former names have been Elm House, The Tree Inn and The Tree Tavern.

The Elm House from a print of 1824, courtesy of Iffley Church. The Tree in the name is after the famous elm tree which had been planted in 1614 and which lived for 350 years until Dutch Elm disease finished it off. A replacement oak was planted in 1974. Tree Lane was once a sheep way and opposite its junction with Church Way stood the village stocks until they were burnt in Oxford to celebrate the fall of Sebastopol in September, 1855.

The old elm tree. (Copyright Jeremy's Postcards)

The Tree Hotel as it is today. The present building dates from the 19th century but it replaced at least one earlier inn. Thomas Hearne (1678–1735), the Oxford antiquary and diarist, was there in March, 1715/16 and he wrote: '. . . called and dined at Iffley at the Ale-House (kept by one Jackson) by the great elm tree now an 100 years old.' When Jackson died in September, 1725, Hearne recorded that he had been born at Iffley 'at the house by the great elm tree' and that a nephew of Jackson's was still living there and 'keeps the public house.' There was an extension built to the north in 1933.

More recent tenants have been Mr and Mrs Wood and family and then Mr Edmund (Eddie) and Mrs Madge Webber who were there from 1946 to 1962. Before this, the Webbers kept one of the village shops.

Eddie and Madge Webber in the garden of the Tree Hotel. Eddie died in 1976 but Madge came back there in August, 1988 to celebrate her 90th birthday.

Madge at her party. She said that she was thrilled to see how lovely the hotel was, run by Mr and Mrs Barry Cooke. (Photographs courtesy Mrs M. Webber)

The Webbers used to put on lunches for Morris's staff and Madge remembers Sir Alec Issigonis (1906–1988), the motor engineer and designer, best known for his design of the Morris Minor (1948) and the Mini (1959). She says that he used to draw cars on the table cloth, scribbling as he talked. She also remembers when the F.A. Cup, held by Blackpool, was seen in the bar and the time when Gene Kelly, the singer, and his wife were guests. Egon Ronay also visited and entered the Tree in his Good Food Guide.

The Prince of Wales

Originally a private house, this was opened as an inn by William Mathews on 13th June, 1863. It was renovated in 1975. The extension on the right, which is now known as The Old Bakery Bar, was once the village bakery. Baker's Lane, which consisted of about a dozen cottages, but which no longer exists, would have gone through this extension. The pub was named after the future King Edward VII in about 1870.

Hawkwell House Hotel

The present-day hotel, photographed in 1999. Originally there were two houses one of which was 'Hawkwell', which backed onto Tree Lane, and which was named for Hawkwell furlong, the field on which it was built. It belonged to John Parsons, banker, of the Old Bank in Oxford High Street.

Between Hawkwell and Church Way was 'The Elms'. Once occupied by the Allen family (see Section 10); it later (in the 1970s) became a Co-operative Society hotel. A developer then bought both houses and also 'The Priory', a private residence next door.

More complicated changes concerning the name of the hotel took place when new owners came and enlarged the hotel further. At first they transferred the name 'Priory' to it from the next-door house. Hawkwell had then become staff quarters for the hotel. There was a further alteration in the name when it was called 'Hawkwell House' which included the much-enlarged former 'Elms' and its staff annexe. (Information courtesy of Miss Shiela Fairfield.)

The Isis Tavern

This early 19th century public house, situated beside the towpath across the river from Iffley lock, was once known as the Isis Hotel, and has not changed much over the years.

The Isis Hotel, probably taken in the early 20th century. Note the hayrick on the right and, in the left distance, near the sign, are a chocolate machine and a penny weighing machine. There were also stables and poultry in the early days.

There have been three generations of the Rose family as landlords of the Isis. This is Tom Rose who was landlord between 1927 and 1939. Until then he had been the Donnington ferryman since 1902. For many of the years when the children (five sons and five daughters) of Tom Rose and his wife Rose (née Beechey) were growing up, there were no modern conveniences. Drinking water came from Iffley and they washed off the pub landing stage. There was no electricity until 1949 and only from that year was there a well in the garden.

On Tom's 60th birthday, Lord Douglas Hamilton, when an undergraduate at Oxford, brought 60 rockets to let off at the pub and he played the bagpipes from the pub roof. Since the early days the hotel was a popular place for undergraduates. They had to be alert for the University bulldogs (policemen), because the Proctors did not allow undergraduates to enter public houses. Tom Rose's children were given pennies if they spotted a bulldog. The undergraduates would then escape by the back door and make their way to Cold Harbour in the Hinksey direction.

During the great floods of 1947 the family had to spend 60 days in the upper rooms. Their food was brought by canoe and the chickens were taken up to a bedroom.

Tom won a cup in a challenge football contest against an elephant at Lord George Sanger's circus. No one had thought it possible for anyone to kick the ball past the elephant but Tom did. At the subsequent celebrations a student fired a gun at the cup and the hole is still in it.

People often wonder how the beer was delivered to such an isolated place. It was delivered once a week, down a narrow right of way, just north of Grist Cottage, which was leased by Morrell's. The lorries parked in Mill Lane and the pathway down to the river was just wide enough for two barrels of beer. When it reached the river, downstream of the lock, it was loaded into a wide. flat-bottomed boat and punted across the river, winter and summer.

Coming down the river was a pathway known as Coffin Lane. Because coffins were not allowed to be taken through the toll-gate, the Rose family would some-times help by punting across a coffin from the west side of the water to be carried up this lane to the church.

Bill Rose bringing the beer from a slipway near Donnington bridge (part of which can be seen in this photograph). Once the bridge and slipway were built this was a more convenient way to ferry the beer. On some occasions the boat was pulled by a rope. Bill's dog Bruce is seen in the bows.

When Bill died in 1978 his wife Gwen held the licence until, in 1980, Tom, grandson of the original Tom, took over. The name 'hotel', which Bill and Gwen had retained, despite the fact that it had ceased to be one since 1949, was changed to Tavern by Tom and his wife Caroline. (Above photographs courtesy of Mr Tom Rose.)

The last of the Roses at the Isis. Tom and Caroline left in 1999, thus ending three generations of landlords of the same family. Tom is holding the cup which his grandfather won.

The Isis Tavern as it is today. The ancient yew tree, seen in the garden, has been there for at least two centuries.

A public house called The Five Bells once existed in Iffley. It was situated in the former house of the caretaker of the Memorial Institute (see Section 7).

People

It is not of course possible to mention the names of all the families who have lived in Iffley over the last few centuries. This chapter will, I hope, at least give an impression of the kind of people who have made Iffley their home over the years. In most cases the availablility of photographs has dictated which people are included in the following pages.

The Henwoods

Left: Sarah Lydia Henwood (1872–1940) and right: George William Henwood (1863–1931). (Photographs courtesy of Mr John Phipps) Sarah and George had seven children. At least six generations of Henwoods are buried in Iffley churchyard.

Mr John Phipps in front of his house in Tree Lane in 1999. He is the grandson of Sarah and George (above). His mother Bessie was their sixth child. Other descendants of Sarah and George also still live in Iffley, children of Dolly Henwood.

The Wilsons and Wyatts

Kitty Wilson, wife of Frederick Wyatt with one of her two sons. Kitty was the daughter of Mr and Mrs Joe Wilson. Joe (born 1890) was not only a chorister of St John's College and the village schoolmaster but also the tenant of the the mill (see earlier section). Although the mill was let during Kitty's childhood they lived at the mill house. When the fire of 1908 started, which destroyed the mill, Kitty's mother, who was an invalid, had to be rescued from the house. Kitty herself was returning from school at the time. Kitty's husband, Frederick, had a drapers' shop at Carfax.

The Frederick Wyatts lived at 'Mill Hill', a house in Mill Lane, which was demolished and replaced by 'The Wilderness' in 1973. Mrs Kitty Wyatt (back) in the garden of Mill Hill in about 1929/30 with (left to right: Judy?, Geoff (who played football for Oxford City), Ralph and their Aunt Blanche. The dog's name was Max.

The front of Mill Hill. Centre is Ralph Wyatt with (left) his Aunt Nellie and (right) his cousin.

Ralph Wyatt, in the Navy in about 1945, was born in Iffley in 1922 and still lives there. He attended the village school and went on to Southfield and then Commercial School. When the war came he enlisted in the Royal Navy and joined the Patrol Service which involved minesweeping and anti-submarine. After the war he married Joan (died 1982) who came from Howard Street, Oxford.

Below: Ralph Wyatt outside his home in Iffley with his grandaughter Joanne, one of his six grandchildren. Taken in 1979. All Wyatt photgraphs courstesy of Mr Ralph Wyatt.

The Allens

John Allen (1857–1934) came from Northern Ireland and joined the Cowley firm of Eddison and Nodding as a partner in 1885, becoming manager in 1887. At first he lived at 'Wootten' but moved to 'The Elms' in 1895. In 1897 Allen bought the business from the Eddison family for £13,000. By 1924 the company was known as John Allen and Son.

John Allen at the wheel of his car with his wife and two sons, J J Cullimore, (on the left) born 1895, and George. The photograph was taken outside 'The Elms' in about 1900. John Allen owned the first motor car in Iffley, having bought it in 1900 from the Daimler Car Co. for £416. ll shillings and 6 pence. Mrs Elizabeth Allen, John's wife, was the first lady driver in Oxford. Captain J J Cullimore Allen and Major George G W Allen, M.C. became joint managing directors of the Allen business in Cowley. John Allen retired in 1920.

The Allen family in about 1914. In front are John and Elizabeth Allen. Behind, left to right, are their children, John James Cullimore, Phoebe, and George. The boys are in their army uniform.

George Allen, son of John, owned a Puss-moth plane. He became a pioneer of Aerial Photography, taking photographs with a camera which he made himself. George is seen here talking to his mother. His father and Nurse Kennedy, who was with the family for many years, are seen on the right. Taken in about 1928.

Left to right: George Allen with his father and mother. George was killed in a motor cycle accident in 1945.

All Allen photographs courtesy of Mrs Verena Allen.

The Polleys and the Webbs

Eleanor Kate Polley, née Mander, who lived with her husband and family at Nowell House (see Section 5). She was born at Court House which is between the church and the old school. One of her sons was Mayor of Abingdon.

The wedding of Violet Polley and (George) David Webb in 1936. Violet made her own wedding gown and her mother's dress for the occasion. It was said that when Violet married David Webb all the young men in Iffley went into mourning. Some called her 'The Belle of Iffley'. She had been May Queen at school. Left to right: Mrs Webb, mother of the groom, Mr Webb, father of the groom, David, Violet, Mr Francis Polley, father of the bride, Mrs Eleanor Kate Polley, mother of the bride.

David and Violet Webb on their Golden Wedding Day in 1986. Born in 1906, Violet has seen seven Vicars come and go at Iffley Church. She and David started their married life in Courtland Road and then at Nowell House where Violet had lived before her marriage. Here they joined Violet's mother, Eleanor Kate, whose husband Francis had died on the day the Second World War began, 3rd September, 1939.

Photographs courtesy of Mrs Violet Webb.

The Benfields

The Benfield family in about 1903. Back row (left to right): Lizzie, Jack, Harry. Front row: George Benfield (1848–1918) with William H. Benfield on his knee, George's wife, Mary Ann (died 1934), Fred and Nell. Nell married Walter Dean who made the famous lamp-posts which were installed all over Oxford; some still survive in Iffley. The partnership of the builders George Benfield and W F Loxley started in 1876. In due course George was asked by William Morris (later Lord Nuffield) to find him a site for his factory. This he did and once found, Morris said to George: 'You better build it then'.

There had been three generations of Benfields at the Benfield and Loxley firm until about 1957. The Benfield residence at 18 Abberbury Road (known as 'Sou'west), built in 1927 by William H Benfield (died 1945) was the first house to be built in the road. The house opposite the Tree Hotel was also Benfield-built in about 1900.

Councillor Bill Benfield and his wife at the wedding of Frances Hills and Simon House on 30th March, 1964.

Bill was a model railway enthusiast. He started the railway which was situated on the north side of Abberbury Road in a paddock which had been originally purchased by the Benfields in order to preserve their view of Oxford. He started it in 1960 at the time his son Andrew was born and it continued until 1985/86. When Bill sought planning permission for the model railway, some villagers were concerned about the possible noise. When Bill explained that it would make no more noise than a lawnmower they retorted: 'A lawnmower is necessary. This is not.' In the event it was allowed to go ahead and was a favourite recreation, especially at village fêtes. The trains were real scale models and coal-fired. Now Nos. 13a and 15 Abberbury Road have been built on the site.

Members of the Benfield family with one of Bill Benfield's scale models in about 1967. On the train is Louise Nightingale with her sister Sally, standing (right), behind, Sarah Benfield (centre) and Lucy Benfield in the pram. (Benfield photographs courtesy of Mr Andrew Benfield)

The Cordreys

Edward Cordrey grew up in Iffley, living at Stone Cottages, and went to Iffley school. In later life, he lived not far away in Howard Street. He was a much-loved and respected personality in the village. It has been said that if it had not been for Edward Cordrey the children would never have been given a free outing. On Friday nights he used to record the Thrift Club contributions. This was the way many families saved. At the end of the year an envelope was returned to the family with the due amount saved. Cordrey was a printer at Mowbray's, the church publishers.

In 1956 Cordrey wrote *Bygone Days at Iffley* which, with the earlier history by Marshall, is still much read and treasured by Iffley people. In old age he would come to church services on Sundays and then chat with or visit old friends afterwards.

Here Edward Cordrey is seen by the churchyard wall talking to Mr Tom Collis (to whom the photograph belongs). The date is not known. Cordrey's obituary in June, 1972 stated that he was a much-loved son of the parish whose life was devoted to its church and people. He was one of those 'holy and humble men of heart'.

Miss Jean Cordrey, daughter of Edward, seen here in Iffley as a landgirl during the Second World War. (Courtesy of Mrs I Crisp.)

The Marchants

Mr Edgar Marchant, Fellow of Lincoln College and a Classics don, and his wife Ethel, née Mallett, were married in 1914. They came to Iffley from Oxford just after the First World War and lived at Rosedale until about 1946. They had two sons. The eldest was (Edgar) Vernon, born 1915, who married Joyce Storey and had three children. The younger son, John was born in 1925 and is unmarried.

The Marchant family in the garden at Rosedale in 1934. Left to right: Vernon, Edgar, John and Ethel. Vernon made his own canoe from plans in *The Boys' Own Paper* in about 1924/25 and launched it from the garden near the lock.

The Marchants in June, 1940 a few weeks before John was evacuated to the United States of America.

Two popular Nurses who lived at Box Cottage, now 46 Church Way. Maud Cook is on the left and Miss Hettie Henry is on the right.

The above three photographs courtesy of Mrs Joyce Marchant.

The Palmers

Gerald Palmer and his wife Diana (née Varley) came to Iffley in 1937 and lived for some years at the Thatched Cottage. Their only child, Celia, was born in Iffley.

Gerald designed many famous British cars including the Jowett Javelin, MG Magnette and the Riley Pathfinder. This photograph is on the front cover of *Auto-Architect. The Autobiobraphy of Gerald Palmer* published by Magna Press, Leatherhead, Surrey, 1998, and reproduced with their kind permission. It shows Gerald with some of the cars he designed.

Gerald Palmer at the wheel of his 1924 Targa Florio Mercedes which he restored. The photograph is published with the kind permission of *Classic and Sports Car* . He had a long career in the motor industry including Oxford. After the merger between Austin and Morris, to form BMC, he moved to join Vauxhall. He kept his house in Tree Lane, Iffley (designed by the architect A Harvey) and commuted 92 miles to Luton and back each day for a period of 16 years. Cars were not his only forte; the portable anaesthetic machine which he designed during the Second World War came to be much valued. (Photographs courtesy Mr Gerald Palmer and Miss Celia Palmer.)

Mrs Graham Greene

Shown here, with two of the most important things in her life, her collection of dolls' houses and her cat. Also in the picture is her book *The Vivien Greene Dolls House Collection* . The photograph was taken in March, 1996. Coyright *Daily Mail/Solo* .

Mrs Graham Greene, widow of the author, came to live at Grove House in 1947. She built the Rotunda next to the house which until recently housed her 'baby houses'.

Mrs Graham Greene at home in 1994 entertaining members of the Oxford Cat Club (of which she was President for many years) to a Mad Hatter's Tea Party. Others in the photograph are; back row: third from left, Joyce Hearn, fourth from left, Mrs Elizabeth Martin (who later became chairman of the club). Front row: Ann Symons, Ann Spokes Symonds, −, Nancy Scott. It is not known who is kneeling down in front.

Tenniel's drawing of the Mad Hatter's Tea Party. It is said that Mr T Carter, who owned a furniture shop in Oxford and lived at Grove House from about 1900, was the model for Tenniel's drawing of the Mad Hatter in *Alice in Wonderland*. He was known as the Mad Hatter because he wore a top hat and had unusual ideas.

The Warins

Dr John Warin and his wife Dr Kathleen Warin came to live at Rosedale after the Marchants had moved from there. Dr John was a loved and respected Medical Officer of Health for the City of Oxford. The John Warin Ward at the Churchill Hospital was named after him.

The wedding of John and Kathleen's daughter Marigold to Dr John Thornley in July, 1961. Standing outside the west door of Iffley Church are, left to right: Mr Thornley, Mrs Thornley (groom's parents), Stephen Thornley, Catherine Thornley, the groom, the bride, Eve Warin (Marigold's sister), Dr Kathleen Warin, Dr John Warin.

The Golden Wedding of Drs John and Kathleen Warin in the garden at Tudor Cottage to which they had moved from Rosedale. Left to right, back row: Robert Warin, Eileen Morris, Debbie Thornley, Alice Bruce, Margaret Swallow, Ben Warin, Jo Warin, Ben Thornley, Fiona Warin, Natasha Sutton, Eve Warin, Stella Warin, Andrew Warin. Front row: Lisa Thornley, with Mark Thornley behind her, Ann Warin, John Warin, Kathleen Warin, Malcolm Bruce, Richard Spicer.

The Critchleys

John and Joan Critchley (née Ballard) have played a prominent part in the life of Iffley for over 50 years. An important event was their purchase of the Glebe field on behalf of the village. One of John's most important contributions during his long life (he died in 1999) was the work he did on behalf of small businesses both locally in Oxford and nationally.

John and Joan Critchley on the occasion of their Ruby Wedding in 1971. Left to right, back row: Anna Critchley, Wendy Edwards, Mary Tate (née Critchley), Geoffery Tate, Bob Boorman, Vivien Boorman (née Critchley), Mark Boorman, Roger Critchley. Seated: David Boorman, Simon Tate, Joan Critchley, John Critchley, Emma Tate, Jeremy Boorman.

The Mayalls

The Mayalls at the Manor House where they lived from 1972. Before that they lived at Wood House (now no more). It was in this room at the Manor House that Dr Johnson and Boswell visited the Nowells (see Schools) in 1784 and when the party 'toasted Church and King with true Tory cordiality'. Back row (left to right), Mayall unless otherwise stated: Jack (in chair) and his children Betty, John, Gill and her husband James Fletcher-Watson. Front row: Grandchildren: Charles and Josephine Fletcher-Watson. One can just see the black dog Jasper in the right-hand bottom corner. The photograph, courtesy of Miss Betty Mayall, was taken at Christmas 1990.

The Ritchie Russells

The name of Dr Ritchie Russell, who was Professor of Neurology at Oxford University (died December, 1980) is still well-known in Oxford today. Both Ritchie Russell House on the Churchill site and Ritchie Court in Summertown were named after him. His wife Jean taught art at St Faith's School for 18 years. They lived at Court House for nine years in the 1960s.

The marriage of Helen Russell, daughter of Dr and Mrs Ritchie Russell, to Simon Leslie-Carter on 19th June, 1965. The group, outside Iffley Church, are left to right: Fiona Low, Pamela Low, Gilbert Leslie-Carter (standing behind), father of the groom, Jean Russell, Simon Leslie-Carter, Helen Russell, Dr Ritchie Russell, Melanie Leslie-Carter, mother of the groom, Rene Cannick, best man, Jane Low.

Helen Russell with her new husband, Simon Leslie-Carter and her bridesmaids (left to right) Pamela, Jane and Fiona Low. Note the famous chestnut tree at the entrance to the churchyard. The house behind is Court House which is a listed grade II building probably of 17th century origin.

Photographs courtesy of Mrs Jean Russell.

The Bromleys

Ron Bromley has lived in Iffley since 1954 when he married Freda, a resident of Iffley since 1939.

Mr Ron Bromley with a hearse (horse-drawn) of 1875. Ron established Bromleys undertakers in 1960 and although the firm was sold in 1988, it continues under the same name of Ronald L. Bromley. Ron saw a horse-drawn hearse in Finchley when he was eight years old and had thought ever since that it was the only way to depart this life in style. He bought his hearse in Nottingham and it is known as a city model because of its rubber tyres and jet black paintwork. The plate-glass windows are etched with flowers. The photograph (copyright Ivor Fields) was taken in October, 1970.

The Hills Family

The Reverend Jonathan Hills was Vicar of Iffley from 1959 to 1975. He was much interested in the history of Iffley and made a fine collection of written and pictorial material relating to it.

The wedding of Frances Hills, daughter of the Reverend and Mrs Hills, to Simon House on 31st March, 1964. The groom's parents, Wilfred and Marjory House, formerly of Grove House, Iffley Turn, are seen on the left. The bride's parents, the Reverend Jonathan and Mrs Diana Hills, are on the right. The Reverend Simon House was at

Cambridge and Cuddesdon, as was his father-in-law. The photograph, which was taken outside the west door of the church, courtesy of Iffley Church.